The African American Community in Rural New England: W. E. B. Du Bois and the Clinton A. M. E. Zion Church

Published by:
Berkshire Publishing Group LLC
122 Castle Street
Great Barrington, Massachusetts 01230
www.berkshirepublishing.com

Printed in the United States of America
First published in 2007 under the title *Sewing Circles, Dime Suppers, and
W. E. B. Du Bois: A History of the Clinton A. M. E. Zion Church* by Berkshire
Publishing Group. 2018 edition ISBN 9781933782058 (hardcover) and
9781614720041 (paperback).

Library of Congress Cataloging-in-Publication Data

Levinson, David, 1947–
  The African American Community in Rural New England:
  W. E. B. Du Bois and the Clinton A. M. E. Zion Church / David Levinson.
     p. cm.
  Includes bibliographical references and index.
  ISBN 1-933782-05-6 (alk. paper)
  1. Clinton A.M.E. Zion Church (Great Barrington, Mass.)—History.
  2. Great Barrington (Mass.)—Church history. 3. Du Bois, W. E. B.
(William Edward Burghardt), 1868-1963. I. Title.
  BX8481.G74L48 2006
  287'.87441—dc22
                                    2006031447

The African American Community in Rural New England: W. E. B. Du Bois and the Clinton A. M. E. Zion Church

David Levinson

BERKSHIRE PUBLISHING GROUP

Table of Contents

Publisher's Foreword

This book was first published in 2006 as *Sewing Circles, Dime Suppers, and W. E. B. Du Bois: A History of the Clinton A. M. E. Zion Church*. We had been planning to reissue it with a new title as an ebook when we heard about the Clinton Church Restoration (CCR) nonprofit organization, launched in 2016 to raise funds to purchase the abandoned church and restore it as a community building celebrating local African American history. The author of the book, David Levinson, kindly agreed to write an epilogue to bring the story up-to-date and we are grateful to him for this addition, covering the tragic murder of Rev. Esther Dozier and the church's subsequent closure and restoration efforts.

The new book's title, *The African American Community in Rural New England: W. E. B. Du Bois and the Clinton A. M. E. Zion Church*, was chosen to emphasize that this book provides general readers as well as students with a fresh look at a loving and vibrant community that existed, and still exists, in rural New England and other parts of the United States. The simply told story makes it clear that the African American community, in small towns as well as big cities, has been fundamental to the remarkable intellectual, literary, and political accomplishments of African Americans.

Berkshire Publishing's mission is to promote cross-cultural understanding and global perspectives, and it has always meant a great deal to us that Du Bois grew up in Great Barrington, Massachusetts, the small New England town where Berkshire was founded. Berkshire Publishing Group is happy to support the work of the Clinton Church Restoration with copies of the book to be used in fundraising, and proud to share this fascinating account of a small but valiant African American community—much of it in the words of W. E. B. Du Bois, one of the great intellectuals of the twentieth century—with readers around the world in this new print and digital edition.

Karen Christensen
Berkshire Publishing Group
December 2017

The opening of W. E. B. Du Bois's *The Souls of Black Folk*, published in 1903:

Herein lie buried many things which if read with patience may show the strange meaning of being black here at the dawning of the Twentieth Century. This meaning is not without interest to you, Gentle Reader; for the problem of the Twentieth Century is the problem of the color-line. I pray you, then, receive my little book in all charity, studying my words with me, forgiving mistake and foible for sake of the faith and passion that is in me, and seeking the grain of truth hidden there.

I have sought here to sketch, in vague, uncertain outline, the spiritual world in which ten thousand thousand Americans live and strive. First, in two chapters I have tried to show what Emancipation meant to them, and what was its aftermath. In a third chapter I have pointed out the slow rise of personal leadership, and criticized candidly the leader who bears the chief burden of his race to-day. Then, in two other chapters I have sketched in swift outline the two worlds within and without the Veil, and thus have come to the central problem of training men for life. Venturing now into deeper detail, I have in two chapters studied the struggles of the massed millions of the black peasantry, and in another have sought to make clear the present relations of the sons of master and man. Leaving, then, the white world, I have stepped within the Veil, raising it that you may view faintly its deeper recesses,—the meaning of its religion, the passion of its human sorrow, and the struggle of its greater souls.

Introduction

Many, many stories make this history. There were Rev. Hatfields's "illustrated sermons" in the 1890s, the camp meetings in Van Deusenville at the turn of the twentieth century, Rev. Morrison's appeal to the selectman for better housing for the Black population, Rev. Dozier's fiery calls for social justice, the comforting music of the choirs, and the program on W. E. B. Du Bois put on by the Jubilee School in June 2001.

It was that Jubilee School program—one of the first events to honor Du Bois in his hometown—that first brought my attention to the Clinton African Methodist Episcopal (A. M. E.) Zion Church. It was organized and hosted by the church and Rev. Dozier, held in St. Peter's Roman Catholic Church hall, and put on by students of the Jubilee School in Philadelphia, which had developed a course of study on Du Bois. The Clinton and Macedonia Baptist Church choirs performed, and Professor David Graham Du Bois, stepson of W. E. B. Du Bois, was the guest speaker.

The event fascinated me as a Great Barrington resident and an anthropologist for a number of reasons: It was hosted by a Black church, but was held in a Roman Catholic facility; it was about Du Bois, but Du Bois was widely ignored in his hometown—in fact, no Great Barrington officials were in attendance. Rev. Dozier of the Clinton Church and Rev. Durant of Price Memorial both gave powerful statements. The audience was a good mix of Blacks and whites. And it concluded with everyone singing "Lift Every Voice and Sing," the African American national anthem, written in 1900 by part-time Great Barrington resident James Weldon Johnson.

This history of a small Black church in rural New England is an unlikely publication for a cultural anthropologist who has spent his career studying global, cross-cultural themes. I began it as a research project I could do in my free time; my original idea was to produce a small pamphlet. But the more I researched, the more the work grew, eventually becoming the book you now hold. Furthermore, as I discovered that this church had much greater significance, both in African American history and in the history of the region, than I had originally imagined, my research efforts expanded; I found myself also working on a guide to the African American community in Berkshire County and undertaking new research on faith in America.

As a secular Jewish academic from Newark, New Jersey, I was surprised by how much my research affected my feelings about the role of religion in community life and by how enriched I felt, thanks to the connection I formed with the church and the African American community in Berkshire County. It has allowed me to experience firsthand a small religious community and has shown me the power of faith and belief in a better future. I've gained insight into the community in which I live. Sadly, one of those insights has been a recognition that things have not changed nearly enough since Du Bois wrote of the color line in 1903, although the new Upper Housatonic Valley African American Heritage Trail is helping to make the often invisible African American community more visible. My experience researching and writing this book has shown me that one result of America's shameful behavior towards African Americans has been a terrible waste of human creativity, strength, and dignity.

Finally, my work on this book—and in particular, hearing Rev. Dozier's sermons and observing the deep faith of those who come together at Clinton A. M. E. Zion Church—has led to a new project, called Faith in America. Faith in America is a compilation of a series of in-depth interviews with people of faith from America's tapestry of faiths that explores what faith means in America and how it shapes and guides people's lives.

Some twelve years ago, when I first started coming regularly to Great Barrington, a town of 7,700 residents in the southwestern corner of Massachusetts, I did notice that the town had a lot of churches on Main Street—Episcopal, Congregational, Catholic, Methodist, and Christian Science, plus two synagogues on side streets. Later, after moving to the town to start a small publishing business, I made occasional trips to the co-op market on Rosseter Street. I noticed that there were two Black churches—the Macedonia Baptist Church on Rosseter and the Clinton A. M. E. Zion Church around the corner on Elm Court. This surprised me; Great Barrington was strikingly white, then as now, and I couldn't understand how there could be two separate Black churches in a tiny section of town. I was later to discover that there had once even been a third.

As I mentioned earlier, it was in 2001 that I began to take real notice of the Clinton Church. We were then working on the *Encyclopedia of African and African-American Religions,* the second book in the multivolume Religion and Society series I was editing for Routledge. One of the articles in the encyclopedia was about the African Methodist Episcopal

Zion Church, and on reading the article I thought of the Clinton Church. I wanted to know how the Clinton Church fit in the broad framework and history of the A. M. E. Zion denomination. As a cultural anthropologist, I wondered what the church meant to its members and how it fit into the wider Great Barrington community. We also wanted a photo of an A. M. E. Zion Church to accompany the article, and Rev. Dozier was kind enough to help us by asking her congregation to gather outside the church after services one bright summer Sunday. It is nice to see that a larger copy of the photo, taken by my wife Karen Christensen, is still displayed in the vestibule of the church.

At about the same time, I also started to read more about W. E. B. Du Bois. Having specialized in urban studies and ethnic relations, I knew of Du Bois's work and, of course, he was mentioned in many articles in the encyclopedia I was editing. I was intrigued by the fact that an intellectual of his stature, and an eminent Black American, had been born and grown up in tiny Great Barrington. But I had no idea of his connection to the Clinton Church. I discovered it while tracing a reference in David Levering Lewis's biography of Du Bois, which took me to a collection of newspaper columns Du Bois had written as a teenager. Those columns frequently mentioned the A. M. E. Zion Society in Great Barrington in the 1880s.

Meanwhile, interest in Du Bois in his Great Barrington was growing, so my interest in the church dovetailed neatly with the interest of others in Du Bois and Black history in the region in general. Eventually, our shared and complementary interests led me to fruitful collaborations with Rachel Fletcher, Bernard Drew, Elaine Gunn, Francis Jones-Sneed, and others.

I am not a historian; my only previous foray into history was a study of the role of the Oneida Indians in the American Revolution that I undertook while a graduate student, which resulted in an article published in the journal *Ethnohistory*. But as I continued with my research, the idea of writing a history of the church began to tempt me. I cautiously asked Rev. Dozier how she felt about such a project. She responded by showing me all that the church had by way of a written history at that point—a single page, created by church members some twenty years ago, which in a short space did a remarkable job of listing some of the church's many pastors and their terms of service. We agreed that a longer history would be nice and proceeded to see what records the church had that might make this possible.

We met several times, and Rev. Dozier hauled out several boxes and bags of records from the church office. We sorted them into boxes by decade and found that they went back to 1936 (the Great Barrington African Methodist Episcopal Zion Society first met in 1870). There was also a copy of a deed from 1914. While I am sure there are church records older than 1936, we never found them. They may still be in someone's attic or basement or may have been moved when a longtime member died and their house sold; I'm hopeful that some may yet surface.

I realized at that point that I would need other sources and that I would have to do a great deal of interviewing. As a result, the book is a product of both historical research, drawing on documents of many types, and ethnographic research, the kind of work cultural anthropologists like me are most familiar with. I looked for other sources in town and beyond that might prove useful. Bernard Drew's town history, *Great Barrington: Great Town Great History,* helped direct me to places that might house useful documents, such as the Mason Library, the Town Hall, and the Registry of Deeds. The Sources section at the end of this book lists and discusses the value of key sources.

Rev. Dozier also gave me a list of people to talk to who knew much about the church and its history. The most important of these proved to be Wray Gunn, a longtime member and former trustee board chairman, but several others provided vital stories, data, anecdotes, and background details.

Early in my research I discovered three things that made writing this book more difficult than I initially expected. First, to provide a reasonably full history of the church, I realized I would have to study and understand the history of Blacks in the region and town and also the history of the town in general. One reason for this was that Black churches like the Clinton Church were usually the primary black organizations, and relations with the white community were mediated through the church or its leaders. Having reached that conclusion, I discovered the second obstacle to writing this book, namely, that Black history in the region is poorly documented compared with white history. For example, before Drew's history, which greatly expanded coverage of the Black community, the Black community was barely mentioned in town or regional histories. Third, I realized that while my training as an anthropologist would help me with the ethnographic task of gathering information by talking to and observing people and social situations, I needed to brush up on historiography, which focuses on finding the right sources of information, evaluating their trustworthiness, and then weaving a chronological account of events.

The task of placing the history of the church in the context of Black regional history and the history of Great Barrington was made easier than it otherwise would have been by Bernard Drew's town history (mentioned above), which provided important context and clarification of names and places and events, and by my being the editor of *African American Heritage In the Upper Housatonic Valley,* which gave me early access to a great deal of information on African American history and life in the region. This left me with more time to devote to my primary research in the church's records and at Mason Library and Town Hall.

What I have ended up writing is more a social and economic history of the church and relations between the church and other organizations and institutions than it is a history of the religious aspects of the church. I have also made a strong effort to provide details on the pastors and leaders of the church. Regarding religion, I was eventually able to compile a full list of the pastors of the church from 1870 to 2006, but because documents describing religious practice in detail do not survive, I have not been able to document the early religious life of the church or how it has changed over time. For example, it would be informative to be able to compare the practice of the church in its early years with that of the United Methodist Church around the corner; unfortunately that was not possible.

The story of the Clinton Church is a rich one, filled with fascinating details, unique personalities, a few intrigues, and some surprises. For example, there was the Literary Society formed in the 1880s, which organized readings for the membership and the wider community. And then there was Rev. Chauncey Hatfield, a professional photographer (a photo of his is the lower half of this book's cover), who Rev. Dozier was surprised to hear, burned himself to death in 1895 when his "projector" caught his clothes on fire in the church. And the several activist pastors—Rev. Watkins in the 1890s, Rev. Morrison in the 1940s, Rev. Durante in the 1960s, and Rev. Dozier today? And who can forget the story of the men of the church in 1950 digging out the basement by hand to convert it into the social hall still used today. These stories and the many others are illustrated with photographs of people, places, church events, and copies of important documents.

There are a number of people I want to acknowledge and thank for their help. First, needless to say, is Rev. Esther Dozier, who shared perhaps every last piece of paper and photograph relating to the church that was in the church's possession. She also answered numerous questions, both general and specific, about who, what, where, when, and why. Bernard Drew answered questions about town history and about what happened when and where. Wray Gunn provided much information and many insights about the church and the African American community, especially from the 1940s into the 1960s. The map he drew of the Rosseter Street neighborhood showing who lived where and when was most helpful early on in orienting me to the landscape. Several other people, including Elaine Gunn, Henry Dozier, Fran O'Nelll, Lila Parrish, and Rachel Fletcher helped with specific details.

Also of great importance were the people (members and nonmembers, visiting pastors and speakers, and visiting choirs) who attended services and events at the church. How they prayed and sang and what they said added to my understanding of the church and its value to members and the wider community. I remember well the Sunday morning service I attended with our friends Ed and Nancy Beauchamp from Hawaii, a truly meaningful experience both for the Beauchamps and for Rev. Dozier. Sadly, Ed, a well-known scholar of global education who was intrigued by the church's connection with Du Bois, passed away this May.

I also want to thank several people who helped turn the manuscript into this book: Sharon Wirt and Francesca Forrest, who did the copyediting; Ron Toelke and Barbara Kempler-Toelke, who designed the pages and composed the book; Mary Bagg, who proofread; Peggy Holloway, who compiled the index; Joe DiStefano, who designed the cover, and Marcy Ross who coordinated production. I also want to thank Gary Leveille for allowing me to use Rev. Hatfield's photo on the cover.

Finally, I want to thank two members of my family who provided great support during this project. My daughter Rachel attended many events at the church with me and generously shared her observations and insights. And my wife, Karen, I thank for providing encouragement and support throughout, for taking several photos for the book, and for providing valuable advice on how best to present this history.

David Levinson
Great Barrington, 2007

Key Events in the History of the Clinton A. M. E. Zion Church

1860s The A. M. E. Zion Society in Great Barrington holds its first meetings.

1870 First known meeting of the Great Barrington A. M. E. Zion Society takes place in Great Barrington.

1870s The Zion Sewing Society is formed by the women of the Zion Society.

1871 The Zion Society purchases a building lot for a church on south Main Street.

1883 In April, W. E. B. Du Bois writes his first column for the *New York Globe,* reporting Zion Society activities.

The Literary Society is formed.

1884 The Mite Society is formed.

The Zion Society is reorganized and incorporated. It sells the property on south Main Street and purchases property on Elm Court.

1886 In October the cornerstone for the church is laid on the Elm Court property.

1887 The Clinton African Methodist Episcopal Zion Church on Elm Court is dedicated on 6 February.

1887 The Clinton Battalion is formed to raise funds to pay off the mortgage.

1888 The Parish Aid Society is formed by the women of the church.

1889 The church participates in a union service with the Congregational and Methodist churches.

Rev. J. F. Waters inserts himself into local politics when he offers a sermon supporting the building of a community casino (meeting hall) in town.

1890 The church hosts a New England Supper attended by over 400 people.

1892   A subscription campaign is initiated to reduce the church's debt, and the debt is reduced from $1,000 to $498.

1893   The trustees place an announcement in the *Berkshire Courier* thanking the community for its support and asking for additional support to retire the debt.

1894   W. E. B. Du Bois delivers a talk entitled "Some Impressions of Europe" at the church to help raise funds for the church.

Popular entertainers Little Bessie, Dr. J. H. Manley, and "Blind Tom, No. 2" perform at the church.

1895   Reverend Chauncey Hatfield exhibits his new projector.

The A. M. E. Zion Sabbath schools of the New England District hold their annual convention in Great Barrington.

1896   Reverend Hatfield is severely burned while using his projector and dies a week later.

Church founder Manuel Mason's restaurant is destroyed in the Railroad Street fire. The family relocates to Springfield.

1898   Bishop J. W. Hood lectures and preaches in the church.

1899   A revivalist camp meeting is held in July–August.

1900   Another successful series of camp meetings is held.

1902   The church is damaged by scandal when Rev. John LeChia leaves town owing to financial irregularities in his management of church and personal funds.

1904   Presiding Bishop J. W. Hood visits the church.

1908   The church enjoys a revival of membership and its finances under Rev. David Overton.

1911   Longtime trustee Jason Cooley dies at the age of 74.

1913   The church ends its affiliation with the A. M. E. Zion Church and becomes the Second Congregational Church of Great Barrington.

1914   The church reaffiliates with the A. M. E. Zion Church of America.

1921   The mortgage is paid off.

1923   The church takes out another mortgage.

1925   Longtime member and trustee Jennie Moore dies
at the age of 71.

1928   The second mortgage is paid off.

1930   Longtime member Nelson Piper dies at the age of 67.

1934   Peter Joseph, 3-year-old son of Rev. Maurice T. Joseph, is
killed in an automobile accident in Brimfield, MA.

Announcements of services begin to appear regularly in the
"Church Announcements" listing in the *Berkshire Courier* and
continue into 1936.

1938   The church holds a union service with the Methodist
Episcopal Church.

A fund-raising campaign begins to raise $3,000
to build a parsonage.

1939   The parsonage is built and dedicated in December.

1940   Longtime member and former president of the Missionary
Society, Grace Freeman, dies at the age of 79.

1942   The church raises funds and repairs the church roof.

1943   Reverend Henry Morrison complains to the Board of Selectmen about the substandard housing conditions endured by
many African American residents of town.

1944   A Macedonia Baptist mission opens in Great Barrington,
with several former Clinton members among its founders.

Efforts begin to establish a Moorish Science Temple in
Great Barrington.

The Progressive Club is founded by church members and
becomes active in town social affairs.

1944   Former longtime pastor Byron Scott dies.

1945   The church property on Elm Court is deeded back to the
Clinton Church by the A. M. E. Zion Church.

1946   The pastor Rev. George Green dies on 8 June.

1947   In November Rev. Raleigh Dove and church members

participate in an ecumenical service with six other
Great Barrington churches and synagogues.

1948 In May the choir joins in a recital with seven other local
church choirs.

1949 The Moorish Science Temple closes.

1950 The *Courier* publishes an article on W. E. B. Du Bois
in honor of his 82nd birthday.

Longtime member and local preacher Fred Freeman
dies on 7 August.

1951 The basement meeting hall and kitchen are completed.

The district conference is held at the church in September.

1952 The basement is dedicated and later is renovated.

1953 The first church bulletin is published.

The church holds it first sunrise service on Christmas
morning.

1954 The church reaches its largest membership with 77 members.

A fire damages the basement on Watch Night.

1955 The Berkshire branch of the NAACP holds its first
South County meeting at the church.

1956 Reverend David Woodson is named minister for migrant
workers in the northern Berkshires by the Massachusetts
Council of Churches.

1958 The Price Memorial A. M. E. Zion Church is founded
in Pittsfield.

1959 More than 100 people attend a special service at the
Great Barrington Congregational Church to observe
Race Relations Sunday and Brotherhood Week.

1960s Several members of the church become active in the local
branch of the NAACP, and the church is used for meetings.

1962 Former pastor Rev. Raleigh Dove dies.

1968 Bishop Stephen Gill Spottswood, bishop of the A. M. E. Zion
Church and head the national NAACP, speaks at the church.

1969   A Human Relations Council is formed in South County, with Clinton trustee Wray Gunn serving as general chairman. Reverend William Durante leads the police relations subcommittee.

1970   Former pastor Alexander W. Johnson dies.

1973   The church begins a public fund-raising effort to undertake renovation and to add an addition to the church.

1974   The church is transferred to the Boston district of the A. M. E. Zion Church.

Former pastor William Durante dies.

1975   The church is remodeled.

Mrs. Pinkie Brooks, "Mother of the Church," dies.

1975   Trustee Wray Gunn becomes president of Construct, Inc.

1980   The first ethnic fair is held in Great Barrington.

1981   Edna Wilks is honored for her service to the church.

1983   The church celebrates Black History Month for the first time.

1991   Longtime member and officer Mrs. Sinclara Gunn dies.

1994   The church participates in events honoring W. E. B. Du Bois.

1999   Esther Dozier is appointed the first female pastor of the church.

2001   The first annual W. E. B. Du Bois birthday celebration is held.

2003   An interpretive center for the University of Massachusetts Summer Archaeological Field School at the Du Bois Homesite is set up at the church.

2006   The church joins with other organizations to found the Friends of the Du Bois Homesite.

2007   Death of Esther Dozier.

2008   The church is listed on the National Register of Historic Places.

2016   The church is decommissioned.

2017   Clinton Church Restoration purchases the property.

†

CHAPTER 1

Founding and Early Years

The Clinton African Methodist Episcopal Zion Church in Great Barrington, MA, has been heart and soul (or the center) of the black community in this small New England town since 1870. Blacks had lived in town since 1700s, but until the founding of the Clinton Church, they attended white churches — some, in fact, objected to a separate black church. The Clinton Church has become a source not only of spiritual succor to its members but of historical and cultural importance to the wider community.

The black population of Great Barrington remains a small, nearly invisible minority in a town that is increasingly driven by the desires of wealthy second home owners from New York City region. In spite of the changes of the 21st century, the church, led today by Pastor Esther Dozier, retains its importance as the core institution of the Black community in Great Barrington and the southern Berkshires. W. E. B. Du Bois, the eminent intellectual and social activist who grew up in Great Barrington and wrote about the church as a teenager, explained in his *The Souls of Black Folk* in 1903 that:

> *The Negro church of to-day is the social center of Negro life in the United States, and the most characteristic expression of African character. . . . Thus one can see in the Negro church to-day, reproduced in microcosm, all the great world from which the Negro is cut off by color-prejudice and social condition.*

Du Bois experienced this as a boy and teenager in Great Barrington, and as he returned to the town throughout his long life (he died in 1963,

1

on the eve of the March on Washington). Du Bois knew as well as anyone that the Clinton Church was the heart of the black community here, with its literary, children's, missionary and other societies-among them the Ladies' Sewing Circle and the dime suppers that raised the funds which built the church on Elm court, paid the pastors, and kept the building warm in the cold New England winters.

Great Barrington is a small town in Berkshire County in southwestern Massachusetts. Its tranquil neighborhoods stretch north and south on both sides of the Housatonic River and its turn-of-the-20th-century Main Street is a popular stopping point along Route 7, which extends from southern Connecticut to Vermont.

At the time of the church's founding in 1870, only two years after Du Bois's birth, the region was transitioning from farming to the textile industry, and to the tourism which Great Barrington and the Berkshires are known for today. (In fact, some Blacks who settled here first came as servants to wealthy white families who spent the summers in the area.) Although not the first Black church in the Berkshire County (the Second Congregational Church in Pittsfield was founded in 1847), the Clinton Church building on Elm Court (dedicated in 1887) is the oldest building in continual use by an African American organization in the county, and the first institution established by and for Black people in Great Barrington.

In a sermon at the church in September 2005, the visiting Rev. Nathaniel K. Perry described the Clinton Church as, "Grandma's church." This meant, he said, a church that is a refueling place, where members believes that prayer changes things and share a fervent desire to praise God. The Clinton church has always been Grandma's church, as members and visitors today confirm through their praise of the Lord, welcoming of guests, and service to the community.

Another striking characteristic of the church from its beginnings to today is the crucial role played by women. In the church records as well as newspaper accounts we read over and over again of the contributions of the women members. Mrs. Elaine S. Gunn, a longtime Stockbridge and Great Barrington resident, recounted recently how the women of the church like her mother-in-law Florence Gunn raised money, held tag sales, and cooked for the church suppers on almost a non-stop schedule.

2

Throughout its history, the church has emphasized instilling moral values in its children. This includes formal education through Sunday school and the less formal role played by church members who served as role models and who taught the children how to behave. Mrs. Mary Bridgemahon, daughter of former pastor Alexander Johnson (s. 1951 – 1954), recalled how when she was girl no one dared cross Mrs. Pinkie Brooks, the "Mother of the Church," who kept the children in line in church. The pastors and members of the church have helped others through social service work and social activism and have served on the boards of the Historical Society, Construct, Inc. and other civic organizations. Despite being far from a wealthy church, members often did all they could to help the less fortunate in Great Barrington such as nursing home shut-ins, and were much involved in the struggle for civil rights in the 1950s and 1960s and have been active in promoting the legacy of W. E. B. Du Bois for the past several years.

Background on the Clinton Church in the African Methodist Episcopal Zion Church

The Clinton A. M. E. Zion Church is one of the nearly 3,000 member churches that form the African Methodist Episcopal Zion Church. The following brief history and description of the church is based on an article originally written by Sandy Dwayne Martin and published in 2001 in *The Encyclopedia of African and African-American Religions*.

In the United States the A. M. E. Zion Church is one of the seven major independent Black denominations. Its roots are in evangelical Christianity, Methodism, and discrimination faced by Blacks in predominantly white Christian churches in the North. Black people formed their own churches to escape the racism of these white churches. White churches typically barred Blacks from leadership positions and the pastorate, sought few Black members, and, in the case of some, supported slavery.

The A. M. E. Zion Church began in 1796 when several Black members became dissatisfied with the discrimination they encountered in their predominantly white Methodist Episcopal Church congregation in New York City. Leaving the church, they formed an independent congregation, which at first continued its affiliation with the mother denomination. It became an independent congregation in the 1820s, calling itself the African Methodist Episcopal Church. Zion was added to the name in 1848 to avoid confusion with the African Methodist Episcopal Church founded in Philadelphia. James Varick of New York was the first superintendent, a title for church leaders later changed by the church to "bishop."

The church grew steadily but slowly prior to the Civil War. During the 1850s it split into two factions, but in 1862 the rift was healed and the A. M. E. Zion Church, along with other Black Methodist and Baptist churches and some white denominations, aggressively sought converts in the South. The church grew rapidly from approximately 5,000 members in 1860 to about 700,000 by 1916, with most in the South. Like other Black denominations, Zion also attracted members in the western territories that had become part of the United States. Evangelization was less intense in the North, but new churches were founded in New York, New Jersey, Connecticut, Rhode Island, and Massachusetts.

Since its early years, the church has been called the "Freedom-Church," because so many abolitionist, antislavery, and civil rights activists were members of or associated with the denomination. Among these were Sojourner Truth, Harriet Tubman, Frederick Douglass, Jermain Loguen, James W. Hood, William Howard Day, and Alexander Walters. Bishop Walters was a major force along with W. E. B. Du Bois and others in founding the National Association for the Advancement of Colored People (NAACP) in 1909. Bishop Walters was also one of the three vice presidents of the NAACP. Harriet Tubman helped to develop the Underground Railroad. It is possible that a station of the Underground Railroad was located in Great Barrington in a barn and connected cave across the railroad tracks and a few hundred yards to the south of where the Clinton Church was built in 1886. This activist tradition was followed by the founding of the Clinton Church, with frequent discussion of Black-white community relations and several pastors fighting for local housing rights and equal opportunity. In the 1960s it was Reverend Durante of the Clinton Church who led the local movement against discrimination in Great Barrington.

In 1899 Meriah Harris wrote in the Zion journal (p. 22), "That woman, the gentler half of God's creation, was an important, even though invisible, factor in the pioneer work of the Church cannot be doubted." This was certainly true for the Clinton Church. While the male pastors and other men (Jason Cooley, Manuel Mason, Daniel Brown, Egbert Lee, Fred Freeman, Wray Gunn, among others) were the leaders in public, it was the women who cooked the food and ran the church suppers and organized the entertainment that raised money to pay the pastor and erect the church building. The importance of women in the new church is indicated by the deed for the 1884 purchase of the Elm Court property. It was witnessed by five couples: Jason and Almira Cooley, Manuel and Emily Mason, Daniel and Sarah Brown, Egbert and Rebecca Lee, and Jefferson and Margaret McKinley.

The A. M. E. Zion Church was among the very first American denominations to ordain women as elders (full ordination to the pulpit ministry) when Bishop Charles Calvin Pettey, with the approval of the Baltimore and Philadelphia Annual Conference, ordained (Mrs.) Mary Small in 1898. Julia Foote and Florence Randolph also served as pulpit ministers, and during the 1890s there were a number of women activists in the church, including Sarah Pettey, an early feminist who supported women's equality in church and society. The Clinton Church has participated in this tradition, as demonstrated by the many women active in the church and serving as officers since its founding and by the current (as of 2006)

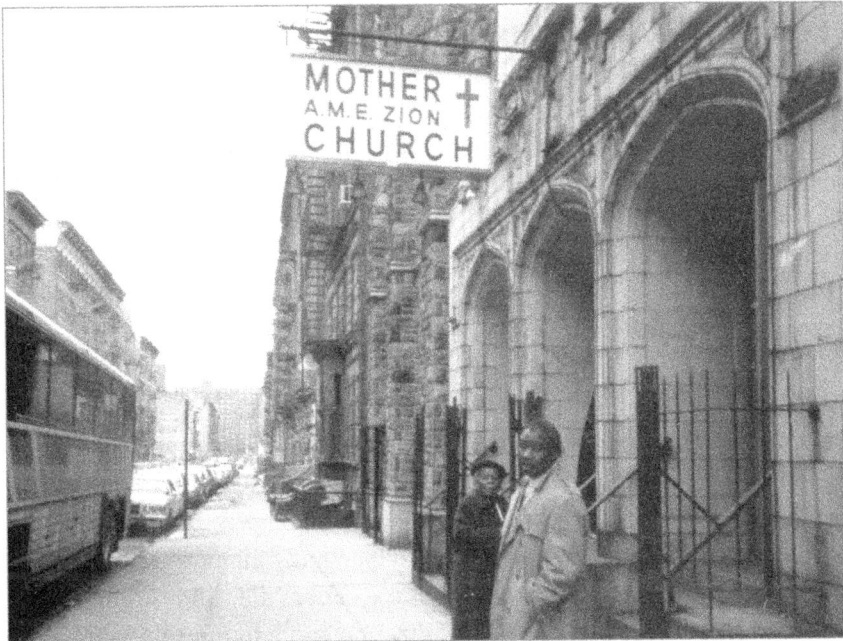

In the 1990s, the church made a trip to visit the Mother A. M. E. Zion Church in New York City. Source: Clinton A. M. E. Zion Church archives.

pastor, Rev. Esther Dozier, who has served since 1999. The Rev. Fanny Cooper of Pittsfield founded the Price Memorial A. M. E. Zion Church in her home on Columbus Avenue in Pittsfield in 1958. It continues to flourish in 2006 and has a close relationship with the Clinton Church. The Warren Brown Chapel, A. M. E. Zion, started by Reverend Cooper in North Adams, Massachusetts, in 1977 has not survived.

In the late nineteenth and the early twentieth century, the church embraced the Holiness movement, which developed in the South in the middle of the nineteenth century and spread from the Azusa Street Revival (1906–1909) in Los Angeles around the world. Many leading A. M. E. Zion bishops at the time supported the movement, and changes in the religious practices at the Clinton Church in the early 1900s suggest that the impact of the Holiness movement was felt in the Berkshires as elsewhere.

As of this writing, the A. M. E. Zion Church has about 2 million members, making it the second-largest Black-affiliated Methodist denomination. The church is divided into twelve districts, with the Clinton Church in the Northeastern Episcopal District. Its schools are Livingstone College and Hood Theological Seminary in Salisbury, North Carolina; Clinton Junior College in Rock Hill, South Carolina; and Lomax-Hannon Junior College in Greenville, Alabama. Overseas schools are A. M. E. Zion Community College University in Monrovia, Liberia, and Hood-Speaks Theological Seminary in Nigeria. Much of the church's operational activities, including its publishing house, are headquartered in Charlotte, North Carolina. Zion has twelve active and five retired bishops. It publications include *The Star of Zion* newspaper and the *AME Zion Quarterly Review.*

Great Barrington from the 1860s to the 1880s

In 1860 Great Barrington was home to 3,871 people; the population rose to 3,920 in 1865 and 4,375 in 1875. As the population grew and new businesses opened, the town slowly expanded north and south along Main Street, above the east side of the river, and west up the Hill. The main industries were the textile and paper mills along the Housatonic, most notably Berkshire Woolen, Owen's Paper Mill, and Waubek Mill, which began expanding as industrialization came to the southern Berkshires in the 1850s. The retail sector also thrived, since Great Barrington served as the market town for the southern Berkshires, and the local economy was beginning to benefit from the seasonal tourist trade. Nearly all the town's residents were white, and most were Protestants, with the Episcopal and Congregational churches the oldest and most prominent.

In the 1850s the social fabric diversified as Irish, German, and, later, eastern European and Italian immigrants arrived to work in the expanding mills. Although these immigrants were poor and uneducated, the mill-work gave them some economic stability, and Great Barrington's schools provided an education for their children. By the 1880s the Irish had become a visible political, economic, and religious force in town. The annual town meeting and the agricultural fair were the highlights of the political and social year, and temperance was the social issue of the day, evidently supported by many, despite the rough bars of Railroad Street. There were social distinctions based on class and race, but all in all, life was quiet and pleasant in Great Barrington. Crime was not a major issue, the poor and ill were cared for by family or other townsfolk, the high school graduated a class each year, and jobs were there for those who wanted them.

But the years from the 1850s into the 1880s were decades of much economic and social change in Great Barrington. Industrialization and the growth of mills accompanied a decline in small-scale agriculture, a change in ethnic composition of the population, and a movement of people from farms into town. While service and craft operations that served the regional economy continued, they were now secondary to the industrialized mills and their wealthy owners.

The Black Community

The African-ancestry population of Great Barrington has always been relatively small. W. E. B. Du Bois remarked in his autobiography, "The other minority in my town were my own colored people, but they were few in number. In Great Barrington there were perhaps twenty-five, certainly no more than fifty, colored folk in a population of 5,000" (Du Bois 1968, 80). Town and church records indicate that the population was somewhat larger than Du Bois recalled, although these records are not to be fully trusted, especially for information about the Black population. In her doctoral dissertation, Nancy Muller (2001, 43) reports the following population figures:

```
1830 .................. 75
1840 ................ 119
1850 ................ 123
1860 ................ 149
1870 .................. 93
1880 ................ 123
```

Many of these were kin—by blood or marriage—of the extended Burghardt family, including Du Bois himself. Other members of the Black community carried the surnames of Townsend, Newport, Piper, Freeman, Bates, McKinley, Cooley, Van Allen, Ferris, Deale, and Walker. Although Great Barrington was the largest town in the southern Berkshires, its Black population was at times not much larger or was even less than neighboring towns. For example in 1870 Lee counted 128 Black residents, Lenox 93, Stockbridge 76, and West Stockbridge 37.

The population decline from 1860 to 1870 reflected the out-migration of Black men and their families seeking employment and opportunity in the Midwest, elsewhere in New England, and in the South. The decline of small-scale farming and discrimination in hiring practices of the mills meant few viable jobs for Black men in the southern Berkshires. This decrease also reflects the service of twelve men from Great Barrington in the all-Black 54th Massachusetts Volunteer Infantry Regiment during the Civil War. Two died (Francis J. Jackson and Levi H. Jackson), and a third (James H. Jackson) went missing in action. Of the other nine, not all returned to town after the war.

The increase from 1870 to 1880 owed to the arrival of Blacks from the South who came to work in the tourist industry. There were also shifts in the age of the population beginning to emerge by the 1880s, with many younger people (like Du Bois) leaving the community to live with and raise their families elsewhere. By the end of the century, many members of the Black community were elderly women, often widows, and this was to have a major impact on the church.

There were significant changes during these decades in the type of work Blacks found in Great Barrington, reflecting the transformation of the regional economy from agrarian to industrial. The U.S. Manuscript Census shows that in 1850 only 5 percent of Blacks worked as domestics or in hotels; by 1870 it was over 30 percent. In 1850, 75 percent of Black women were housewives and only 20 percent worked as domestics in white homes. By 1870 the percentages were 60 percent housewives and 40 percent domestics. As for the men, information on the twenty-eight men who enlisted in the 54th Regiment in 1863 from Great Barrington, Sheffield, and Stockbridge indicates that fourteen were laborers, ten were farmers, two were waiters, and one each, butcher and carpenter. Over the next two decades, the number of farmers decreased and laborer became the occupation of most Black men.

Despite its small size, the Black population was not a homogeneous mass. Du Bois again provides the details:

> *My family was among the oldest inhabitants in the valley. The family had spread slowly through the county intermarrying among cousins and other black folk, with some, but limited infiltration of white blood. Other dark families had come in and there was intermingling with local Indians. In one or two cases there were groups of apparently later black immigrants from Africa, near Sheffield, for instance. Surviving also was an isolated group of black folk whose origin was obscure. We knew little of them but felt above them because of our education and economic status. (Du Bois 1968, 83)*

Joining these groups were the newcomers who came from the South and from northern cities such as New York and settled in Great Barrington beginning in the late 1860s. Some were former slaves or children of slaves, and others were employees or former employees of white families in the North. They were but a few dozen in the massive migration of Blacks to the North in the middle years of the nineteenth century, but several of these men and women took a central role in the founding of the Clinton A. M. E. Zion Church.

In his columns in the Black newspaper the *New York Globe* (later called the *New York Freeman* and, later still, the *New York Age*) from April 1883 to May 1885, Du Bois mentions many members of the Great Barrington community. The following list is hardly complete, since Du Bois mentions mainly people actively involved in the Zion Society and related organizations. The use of *Miss* and *Master* indicate that the named persons are children, while single women have no title.

Austin, Elijah

Austin, Mr. A. W.

Bowen, Mrs. Josie

Brown, Mr. Daniel

Burghardt, J. T.

Chinn, William

Cooley, Jason

Corning, Sarah

Crosley, Miss Delphine

Crosley, William

Dennis, Mr. J. C.

Du Bois, W. E.

Ferris, John

Freeman, Miss Grace

Gardner, Miss Inez

Gardner, Mrs. Lucinda

Gardner, Mrs. S.

Hicks, Miss C.

Jackson, C. F.

Jackson, George S.

Jackson, Gracie

Jackson, Henry

Jackson, Master George

Jackson, Miss Lulu

Jackson, Mrs. C.

Jackson, Mrs. G.

Jackson, Mrs. H.

Jackson, Mrs. J. H.

Jackson, Mrs. Mary

Lee, Egbert

Lee, Mrs. Egbert

Mason, Master Walter

Mason, Miss Francis

Mason, Mr. Manuel

McKinley, Mr. Jefferson

McKinley, Mrs. Jefferson

Moore, Mrs. J.

Newport, Frances

Newport, Mrs. M.

Phillips, Edward

Piper, Anna

Piper, Louise

Piper, Mrs. M.

Piper, William

Sumea, Fred

Sumea, Hattie

Sumea, Miss Jennie

Van Allen, Mrs. M.

Williams, Mrs. J. B.

Wooster, Edward C.

Wooster, Lucinda M.

Wooster, Miss Bertha

Wooster, Miss Florence

Young, Lizzie

Over the next fifty years or more, many of these people, their children, and grandchildren maintained their ties to the Zion church. Among the names that continue to appear for several generations among the church's membership are Brown, Cooley, Crosley, Ferris, Jackson, Mason, Piper, Sumea (or Suma), Van Allen, Williams, and Wooster. Many of those on this list and involved in the church were Burghardts and kin of Du Bois—Freeman, Gardner, Jackson, Newport, Piper, and Wooster. Lucinda Gardner, Du Bois's aunt, was a leader of the church as was Lena Wooster (his mother's first cousin) several years later. Du Bois spent his childhood and teenage years living with and surrounded by men and women and children of the Zion Society, although he and his mother attended the Congregational Church, as had a few other Burghardts in previous generations. Another Du Bois relative who was active in the Zion Church was his cousin Eliza Ann Gardner (1831–1922), who lived in Boston. She was a leader of the Daughters of Confederation of New England and a vice president of the Women's Home and Foreign Missionary Society. An abolitionist and women's rights advocate, she was well connected in Black Boston society and introduced Du Bois to her circle when he was a student at Harvard in the 1890s.

What was life like for these folks of Great Barrington? What we know comes mainly from the writings of W. E. B. Du Bois. He devotes many pages of his autobiographies to his boyhood and adolescent years; of even more historical importance are the dispatches he wrote on the Great Barrington community for the *New York Globe. The Globe,* and its successors, the *New York Freeman* and the *New York Age,* were founded and edited by T. Thomas Fortune (1856–1928), the most influential Black journalist and editor of the late nineteenth and the early twentieth century. Born in Florida and educated at Howard University, Fortune founded the *Globe* as a newspaper for Blacks in the Northeast. The emphasis was on national news, but space was left for reporting on local communities, of the sort provided by Du Bois. The Age, which Fortune edited for over twenty years, was a major voice for Black rights and freedom, and Fortune himself was involved in founding the Afro-American League in 1890, an effort at Black unity and activism that preceded the Niagara Movement and the NAACP.

What Du Bois tells us is supplemented by additional information and interpretation provided by Du Bois's major biographer, David Levering Lewis, and by Great Barrington town historian Bernard Drew in his town history. Information in the town records for the 1860s and 1870s is slim. Coverage of the Black community in the *Berkshire Courier,* the weekly town newspaper, was sporadic in these early years; evidently, the disposition of the editor toward the Black community determined how much coverage it received, although once the church was established in the 1880s, there was much coverage of church events.

Du Bois described his childhood in Great Barrington as "a boy's paradise," but he also learned about distinctions based on wealth and social class, and he experienced the "veil," or the "color line," that separated

Blacks from whites. That experience spurred him in his lifelong effort to pull down that veil and erase the color line. Despite the separation and discrimination, Great Barrington's Black community went back several generations, and many of the people had lived their entire lives in town. And, while poorer than most whites and excluded from some activities (such as employment in the mills or by town government), Blacks clearly saw themselves as part of the community and had a place in it. This perception was based on the day-to-day reality of life in Great Barrington. If they so desired, they could send their children to the public schools that were formed in the 1860s, and a few children also attended white academies. They voted and attended the annual town meeting (but were not active politically in other ways), owned property, and shopped with their white neighbors in the stores on Main and Railroad streets.

Before the establishment of the A. M. E. Zion Society and then the Clinton Church, Blacks who attended church did so at the white churches, and some continued to do so after the Society began meeting regularly in 1870. The earliest recorded Black church member in Great Barrington was "Simon. a Negro," who joined the First Congregational Church on 25 May 1746. The records show that he joined the same day as a Jonathan Willard and that both had joined after leaving another, unnamed church. With slavery still legal in Massachusetts, Simon may have been owned by Willard. Later Black members of the Congregational Church were Dimmis Bunkers (1826), John Van Horsen (1827), Lucinda Freeman (1840), Lucinda Gardner (1865; previously a member of the Methodist Church), and Mary Burghardt Du Bois and William Du Bois (1868). Buried out of the church (their funeral service was conducted by the Congregational minister) and possibly members were Jesse Auguste (died 1829), Joseph Bradley (died 1831), and John Burghardt (died 1832). Members of the Congregational Church in South Egremont, Massachusetts, were Phoebe Freeman (1866) and Althea Burghardt (1871). A member of the Episcopal Church in Great Barrington was Guy Charleton Ray (1821) and buried from the church were Ray (1862), Emma Grace Burget (1871), Ira Burget (1871), and Othello Burghardt (1872). Burget is likely a misspelling in the church records of *Burghardt*. There were Black and white Burghardts in the southern Berkshires at the time, and incomplete records make it difficult at times to distinguish who was who.

In the nineteenth century, and probably the eighteenth as well, at least some Blacks were buried in Great Barrington's Mahaiwe Cemetery (then known as South Cemetery). Most were buried in unmarked graves in two "Negro plots," a larger one at the bottom of the hill and a smaller one at the south end of the cemetery. No markers survive in the larger plot, save for a white marble cross marking the grave of Burghardt Du Bois (W. E. B. Du Bois's infant son buried there in 1899, the stone added later) and a stone marking the 1950 grave of Nina Gomer Du Bois (W. E. B.'s wife). Several stones are extant in the smaller plot, for members of the Burghardt, Piper, Suma, Jackson, and Lewis families, dating from 1849 to 1892. Grave records collected by the D.A.R. in the 1930s and Cynthia Hoog in the 1980s show that the larger plot contains graves for at least thirty-two individuals from the following families: Brown, Wooster, Chinn, Phillips, Jackson, Sumea, Wadhams, Freeman, Goin, Jackson, and Gardner. Several of the men in both plots were veterans of the Civil War: Daniel Brown, Levi Jackson, Francis Jackson, Willie Sumea, J. H. Jackson, and George Suma.

The Black community was limited by discrimination. Blacks had little access to high-paying or stable employment, they had no place in town politics, and they had no church of their own. The relative stability they had enjoyed for generations was threatened in the decades after the Civil War by the influx of European immigrants, who took the better jobs, and by mechanized agriculture and the railroads, which made small farms inefficient and forced men to work in town or as laborers on larger farms. When the Zion Society was founded in 1870, the economic situation of the Black community was precarious.

The Origins of the A. M. E. Zion Church in Great Barrington

As elsewhere in the United States, the A. M. E. Zion Society in Great Barrington provided religious freedom and opportunity unavailable in white churches. While the church was born through the efforts of its founding members, the genesis of the Clinton Church can be found in the convergence of several major national and one regional development in the second half of the nineteenth century. The key national developments were the emancipation of slaves in 1863, the end of the Civil War in 1865, and the migration of many Blacks to the North during and after the war. Regionally the key developments were those mentioned above—industrialization and the demise of small farms as well as the growing popularity of the southern Berkshires as a vacation venue for wealthy and middle-class whites. The wealthy built their "Berkshire cottages," while the middle class enjoyed the cool summer nights on the porches of the Berkshire House at Main and Bridge, the Collins House on Maple Avenue, and the Miller House on Main, among others.

These developments transformed the Black community in the southern Berkshires. The number of Blacks in the region grew, but the population also fluctuated. In 1885 the population was 107—49 men and 58 women, down from 123 five years earlier. The 107 were all described in the Massachusetts census as "native black" with no "foreign black," "native mulatto," or "foreign mulatto" listed. The arrival of the newcomers was noted by Du Bois:

> *The colored population of the town had been increased a little by "contrabands," freed Negroes from the South, who on the whole were well-received by the colored group; although the older group held some of its social distinctions. (Du Bois 1968, 83)*

Why Great Barrington attracted these people is not fully known, but is likely that the growing tourist industry, with its employment opportunities in hotels and restaurants, was an important draw. Another was familiarity with the southern Berkshires gained by those who accompanied their vacationing white employers. Some of these individuals and families then choose to stay or return on their own. The newcomers played a role in the founding of the church. Du Bois comments that "the newcomers astonished us by forming a little Negro Methodist Zion church, which we sometimes attended" (Du Bois 1968, 83). He goes on to provide more detail:

> *Later, and while I was in high school, the colored folk of the town, mostly newcomers, and not old families like the Burghardts, organized a small branch of the A. M. E. Zion church, which had been formed in New York late in the late 18th century. The colored people had long owned a small plot of land in the lower part of town on Main Street. They were induced to sell this for a small plot on a side street, and there they built a*

little chapel. The older Negroes were not at all happy about this segregated institution, but now and then we used to attend the services, which became an inconspicuous part of the religious organization of the community. (Du Bois 1968, 90)

One can well imagine the astonishment of the Burghardts and other old-timers. There had never been, nor does it seem there ever was any great desire for, a church serving just their community. But the newcomers had arrived with a very different set of life experiences and a very different view of the world and their place in white society. Some of them came from the segregated South, where Blacks took care of one another and sought freedom through Black institutions. Churches were primary in this regard. The newcomers for their part were no doubt astonished and even distressed to find no Black institutions to serve them. Founding a church for their fellow Blacks of Great Barrington would have seemed to

Great Barrington c. 1855.

15

them both natural and necessary, so as to have a central institution for their community.

We know from newspaper reports and town histories that both A. M. E. and A. M. E. Zion missionaries were active in Lee, Great Barrington, and Sheffield from the mid-1840s into the 1870s. Their first successes came in Lee and Sheffield, both of which had relatively large and localized Black populations. These new churches followed the development pattern typical of many Black churches. Meetings were at first held in members' homes; then, when the membership increased, in public halls; and finally in a church built by the members.

While the newcomers—through their numbers and desire for a church—played a role in the church, they did not act alone. Old-time families also supplied members; individuals from the Cooley, Burghardt, Ferris, Freeman, Gardner, Wooster, and Van Allen families were among the founders or early members. The two leaders were an old-timer, Jason Cooley, who was born and grew up in Sheffield, and a newcomer, Manuel Mason, who moved to the Berkshires from Virginia with his wife Emily and children in the 1860s. Some old-timers who became involved also maintained affiliation with the Congregational and Episcopal churches in town and the Congregational Church in South Egremont. Not all members of the African American community joined the church, since marriage and burial announcements in the weekly *Berkshire Courier* show white clergy officiating at these rites for some members of the Black community. Summer Black residents—the employees of seasonal tourist facilities and of the wealthy Berkshire cottage owners—were also an important source of members for the new church.

Founding of the Church

There is a good deal of confusion about when exactly the church was founded. Local historian Bernard Drew mentions 1861 and 1870, the MacLean extension of Charles A. Taylor's town history mentions 1888, the church itself lists 1882, and Du Bois mentions 1884 as the key year. The confusion about dates seems to be the result of confusion about what event constituted the founding of the church—when prayer meetings were first held, when the church society was founded, when the church was incorporated, or when the church building on Elm Court was built.

It is also the result of very little information about the formative years of the church. Our limited knowledge is the following. Oral tradition recounted later in the century suggested that the founder may have been an elderly woman in Sheffield known as Aunt Letetia, who raised $20, opened a bank account for the church, and then moved to California. But there is no documentary evidence of this. We know from the Lee town history that Black preachers were active there in the 1840s; in 1844 the Rev. Albert Marie began the work of the African Methodist Episcopal Church in town, and in 1852 the members built a church on High Street. The County Atlas for 1876 shows two Black churches in Lee, one on High Street and the other on Prospect. The origin of the second church is unknown, but it was likely an African Methodist Episcopal Zion Church, there having been an A. M. E. Zion pastor, Cyrus Oliver, in Lee in 1870.

There is no record of communication between members of these churches and the Black community in Great Barrington, although it seems likely that some did take place. It may be significant that Manuel Mason, one of the founders of the Clinton Church, was living in Lee in 1870 before settling in Great Barrington. The *Courier* reported in May 1859 a festival of "colored people" at Sanford's Hall in Great Barrington that raised $28.38. Whether this event had any ties to the church is unknown. In March 1860 another report mentioned a large stone thrown through a window in South Lee while a Rev. D. C. Mitchell was "making a donation visit." It is possible that this is the same Rev. Mitchell identified as the Rev. Jacob Mitchell of New Haven, Connecticut, in the *Courier* on 21 February 1861 (p. 2). In addition to reporting on his slave background and preaching in Europe, the article tells us: "He is a presiding elder in the Methodist Church. His district embraces Norwich, New Haven, and Bridgeport, Ct., Great Barrington and Lee." We also know that a Black preacher, a Mr. Thompson, was in Sheffield in 1867, through a letter from town resident Edward Augustus Croslear to the *Courier* on 21 November 1867. As Croslear later became a deacon in the short-lived A. M. E. Church in Sheffield, Reverend Thompson was likely of that denomination. Finally, the 1860 census lists a Black Methodist minister, William Desmond, and his wife Eveline and four children (Jarvis W., William II, Laura J., and John A.) living in Great Barrington. But we know nothing more about him. All of these hints are tantalizing yet leave us with a very incomplete understanding of how the church began and who was involved.

Bishop J. J. Clinton. Source: Hood, J. W. (1895) *One Hundred Years of the African Methodist Episcopal Zion Church; or, The Centennial of African Methodism.* NY: A. M. E. Zion Book Concern.

The first public record of the church is a meeting announcement in the 24 August 1870 edition of the *Berkshire Courier:*

*The Methodist Episcopal Zion society of Great Barrington,
under the pastoral charge of Rev. W. J. Dorsey, will hold their
quarterly meeting next Sabbath, August 28th, at the Town Hall.
Services commence at 10½ a.m., at 3 and 7½ o'clock p.m. The
society has, aside from the services of their pastor, been favored
with highly interesting and instructive discourses by Rev. R.
Newman and Rev. E. Scudder of Great Barrington, Rev. Mr.
Germond of New York, and Rev. Mr. Hibbard of Brooklyn. The
society feels very much encouraged, and are [sic] determined
to press on, and by the blessing of God to have a house of their
own to worship in within the next year.*

According to church lore, as passed down by the pastor, Rev. Joseph G. Smith, in a recounting of the church history in October 1886, the first meeting was held on 22 July 1870, and the church society was actually founded some years earlier. The church arranged to hold services in Centre School every other Sunday until they built their own building. On Sunday evening, 16 October 1870, Rt. Rev. J. Y. Clinton delivered a sermon at Centre School. It is likely that the paper misspelled his name and he was the Rev. J. J. Clinton, Presiding Elder of the New England Conference of the church. It is likely, too, that the Great Barrington church is named the Clinton A. M. E. Zion Church after him. Reverend Clinton was an important figure in the church and is profiled in J. J. Moore's, James W. Hood's, and William J. Walls's church histories. He was born in Philadelphia in 1823, received a good private education, and became a preacher at age seventeen. An effective missionary, devoted to the welfare of others, and involved in the Underground Railroad, he was recognized by the church for his talents, and he was appointed a deacon, then elder, superintendent, and finally, in 1864, bishop. He died following a lengthy illness in Atlantic City in 1881. At the Seventeenth Quadrennial Session of the Church in New York City in 1884, he was eulogized as follows:

> *Noble in his personal appearance, Bishop Clinton possessed an equally noble heart. Genial in manner, easy, graceful and commanding in bearing, generous and jovial, and, respectful to all, and especially to the aged; condescending to the poorer and more unfortunate in life, it was by no means strange that he drew around him hosts of admiring friends—both in and out of the church. Large hearted, sympathetic and benevolent, he shared alike in the joys and sorrows, the sunshine and gloom, the prosperity and adversities of his brethren and companions. (Walls 1974, 185)*

Four days after Bishop Clinton's visit, the women of the church began what was to become a sixteen-year effort to raise enough money to erect a building:

The ladies of the M. E. Zion society of Great Barrington (under the pastoral charge of Rev. W. J. Dorsey) will hold a festival on Thursday evening, Oct. 20th, in Miller's Hall, for the purpose of raising means to procure a permanent place of worship. The committee will spare no pains in their endeavors to make the affair agreeable and entertaining to all who may favor them with their patronage. (Berkshire Courier 12 October 1870, 2)

The newspaper editor goes on to comment, "We hope our citizens generally will second their endeavors," suggesting community support for the Zion Society. It is important to note that the church's fund-raising activities throughout its history have typically been quite similar to the fund-raising activities of other churches in town. These events included suppers, ice cream socials, strawberry festivals, bazaars, raffles, plays, musical performances, and dramatic readings, among others. The events were usually more important to the Zion church than to other churches because the Zion church never had wealthy members who could make large contributions.

Efforts to raise money continued in 1871, with a large fair and festival held by the women of the church on 30–31 March in Miller's Hall. The announcement in the 22 March issue of the *Berkshire Courier* promised that "articles useful and ornamental will be for sale, also refreshments, consisting of all the delicacies of the season. Ice cream, oysters, etc., etc. Tickets of admission, 25 cents." The fund-raising efforts were successful enough so that when combined with member offerings, they were sufficient for the purchase of a plot of land for the church on 15 September 1871:

To Build a Church—The colored people comprising the M. E. Zion society of this town have bought a building lot in the south part of the village, nearly opposite Mt. Peter, for $650, upon which they propose to build a church next summer. (Berkshire Courier 20 September 1871, 2).

The land was purchased from Charles Botsford and was on the west side of south Main Street, just past what is today the intersection of Routes 7 and 23. Jason Cooley and Manuel Mason signed the deed as trustees for the society.

Fund-raising efforts continued with a strawberry festival in Park's Hall on 10 July 1872 and another festival on 27–28 March 1873 that "left a net profit of about $100 to go towards building a church edifice" (*Berkshire Courier* 2 April 1872, 2). In September, real progress began, with stonemasons hired to procure the stone for the building and plans to begin construction that fall. However, work did not begin then, and in June 1874 and 1875, strawberry festivals were again held to raise money for the church. (Strawberry festivals were a popular church fund-raising activity; the Episcopal and Congregational churches also held them each May or June.) In 1873 there was a change in pastors, with the New England Conference at Worcester, Massachusetts, appointing Rev. William B. Smith to serve Lee, Great Barrington, and Stockbridge.

For the years 1876–1880 we know virtually nothing about the church, notices of its events no longer appearing in the *Courier.* There are, however, two notable later announcements in the newspaper that bear on the church. On 8 March 1876 the paper notes that "Jason Cooley has purchased a fine building lot on Housatonic Avenue [later renamed East Street], the new street to be opened later this summer on the east side of the river, and is intending to erect a two story dwelling house on it." The house was completed in 1882, one of the first on that side of the river. Cooley and his wife, Almira, were well-liked and respected members of the community (both white and Black), and for many years he served as a trustee of the church. He was born in Sheffield in 1838 and was something of a jack-of-all-trades, running a delivery service, transporting people across the river on his raft, and raising chickens. He also ran a catering service and a food concession at the agricultural fair, and in the 1890s operated a restaurant and ice cream parlor and rented out rooms to Black visitors. Cooley died in 1911 at the age of seventy-four. Almira Cooley was a domestic employed by the wealthy Bigelow family.

The second newspaper mention of note was on 20 October 1880, when Manuel F. Mason was among the men listed as voters for the upcoming election on 2 November. This is the first mention of Mason, who, like Cooley, was a trustee of the church and also actively involved in the Sunday school, which at least some of his children attended. Du Bois remembered the Masons well: "There were the Masons, a family of six, a little uncouth and very religious; but good-hearted, hard work-ers and so jolly. I came to like them very much" (Du Bois 1968, 83). Du Bois implied in his text that the Mason family members (Manuel, Emily and their children) were recent arrivals from the South. The 1870 census shows Manuel Mason living in Lee at that time, nineteen years of age and having been born in Virginia. He first became a mem-ber of the Housatonic Agricultural Society in 1872. Listed as a laborer in the town directory, Mason at one point lived on Church Street and later built a substantial home on the road to the reservoir on the east side of the river. He also was in the catering and restaurant business, but the family moved to Springfield, Massachusetts, when his estab-lishment on Railroad Street was lost in the fire of 1896. His ties to Great Barrington evidently ended in 1900, when he sold his property. The deed shows that three white individuals had provided mortgages for the property.

Cooley and Mason's food at the fair met with approval and was favor-ably commented on by the *Courier:*

> *Mr. Jason Cooley and Manuel Mason have erected a temporary home on the Fair Grounds, where visitors to next week's Cattle Show will find excellent provisions for supplying the wants of the inner man, and the inner man should be well looked after at cattle Show time.* (Berkshire Courier *22 September 1882, 4*)

> *Messrs. Cooley & Mason, will as in years heretofore, have their refreshment booth open during the Fair, and furnish eatables of the best to those desiring. Any one who has ever been to their establishment once will always go a second time.* (Berkshire Courier *30 September 1885, 4*)

Jason Cooley and Manuel Mason were among the first leaders of the church, with Mason remaining active until moving away in 1896 and Cooley until his death in 1911. Both served many years as trustees, and Mason and his family were long active in the Sunday school. That both men's personal affairs were mentioned now and again in the *Courier* alongside those of white citizens suggests that both were well respected. Both owned property in town and were among the few

This birds-eye-view map of Great Barrington in 1884 shows several sites where the A. M. E. Zion met in the 1870s and 1880s: (1) Centre School; (2) William Crosley home; (3) Sumner Hall. Source: L. R. Burleigh, Troy, NY.

Black entrepreneurs of the nineteenth century in Great Barrington. Their contacts in the white community of property owners and bankers was no doubt of much help to the new church in later years as it sold and purchased property, borrowed money, and needed the support of the white community in order to survive and grow.

CHAPTER 2

Building the Church

The 1880s were the most important years in the Clinton A. M. E. Zion Church's history. During the decade the church was reorganized and incorporated, its building on Elm Court erected, and the church established itself a stable religious institution in Great Barrington.

The decade began with the women of the A. M. E. Zion Society continuing their fund-raising efforts and with planning under way for the building. In 1880 Silas Mitchell was the pastor, and he boarded in the Burghardt home on the road to Egremont. The 1881 strawberry festival, held at the end of June at the town hall, raised $30 for the building fund. But a fund-raising supper in December was unfortunately hindered by a winter storm:

> *The supper given last week by the ladies of the A. M. E. Zion
> society, at Town Hall, on account of the very bad weather was
> not as successful as could be wished, they being able to add only
> $20 to their chapel fund as the net results of their labors. They
> intend, sometime during the winter, to give another supper, and
> hope for more auspicious weather. By all means let there be a
> good attendance. (Berkshire Courier 14 December 1881, 4)*

A lengthy article on page 4 of the *Berkshire Courier* on 24 August 1881 made it clear that the Society remained eager to build its church:

This society has for several years been preparing for the erection of a church edifice in this village, and a site has been purchased and timber and underpinning stone procured, and already on the lot. Last week a committee was appointed to confer with a committee selected from other churches consisting of Rev. D. G. Anderson, Rev. E. Scudder, Rev. C. C. Painter and H. T. Robbins, upon the advisability of erecting a building this season, but it was recommended in view of all the circumstances, to postpone the work. The recommendation of the committee has been adopted by the society, and they have decided to wait until next spring, and in the meantime to further complete their preparations. The society is now quite united in their feelings, and have confidence in their ability to carry out their work, provided that they have assistance from our citizens which should certainly be given. Already they have raised nearly $1,000, and considerable amounts are promised provided the project is carried forward to completion.

The land preparation had made the south Main Street land more valuable, and it was eyed by Mary Hopkins, a Kellogg from Great Barrington and the widow of California tycoon Mark Hopkins. Dr. Samuel Camp, acting as her agent, purchased the lot on 18 October 1881 for $1,000. On 1 November the church bought, from Mark Humphrey and Phoebe J. Humphrey for $1,500, another plot of land, this one on an Elm Street extension (now Elm Court), as the site for the church. Elm Street had been cut through from the Congregational Church on Main Street to the railroad tracks in 1869 and was a residential street at the time. Signing the deed for the church were five couples: Jason and Almira Cooley, Manuel and Emily Mason, Daniel and Sarah Brown, Egbert and Rebecca Lee, and Jefferson and Margaret McKinley. These five men plus Edward C. Wooster were the trustees at the time. Egbert Lee was a Civil War veteran and a butler for William H. Gibbons, a summer resident from Savannah, Georgia, who owned a house at the corner of Silver and Maple Streets.

In December 1882 a new pastor arrived to conduct the quarterly meeting—one Rev. J. H. Anderson of Providence, Rhode Island. The meeting was held on 10 December in Park's Hall, with services at ten thirty in the morning, three o'clock in the afternoon, and seven o'clock in the evening. The *Courier* noted that "in the evening Mr. Anderson, who is a young man of marked ability, gave an able discourse." The *Courier* was correct in its assessment of the visiting pastor, James Harvey Anderson already having made a name for himself in the church. He was active in Rhode Island politics and was the first Black man nominated to run for the legislature, although he chose not to do so. Anderson served in three different conferences and was a student of church history and known as a fine preacher. It was also announced that the Rev. Silas Mitchell, formerly in charge of this mission, "has been suspended until the conference, when his case will be decided" (*Berkshire Courier* 13 December 1882, 4). What caused this action is not known and, unfortunately, Reverend Mitchell was not to be the last pastor to leave under difficult circumstances before the decade was over.

Life in the Black Community, 1883–1885

From Du Bois's columns in the *New York Globe*, we know much about life in the community and also about the church during 1883 to 1885. It seems safe to assume that at least some of what Du Bois reports was also typical of church life in earlier and later years as well. Church members often met in member's homes on Sunday evenings for Bible study, and the church community came together, frequently with visitors from nearby towns, for quarterly meetings led by visiting pastors. The pastors presiding over the quarterly meetings mentioned by Du Bois were:

May 1883	Rev. J. H. Anderson, Providence, RI
April 1884	Rev. J. F. Lloyd, Middletown, CT
August 1884	Rev. J. F. Lloyd, Middletown, CT
November 1884	Rev. J. F. Lloyd, Middletown, CT
January 1885	Rev. J. F. Lloyd, Middletown, CT
May 1885	Rev. J. F. Lloyd, Middletown, CT
November 1885	Rev. J. G. Smith, Waterbury, CT

The most active of the church's societies was the A. M. E. Zion Sewing Society, which meet weekly and also held monthly suppers. The officers of the Sewing Society for 1883–1884 were:

President ....Mrs. M. Van Allen
Vice President ....Miss C. Hicks
Secretary...............Mrs. Josie Bowen
Asst. Secretary ....Mrs. George Jackson
Treasurer ....Mrs. Lucinda Gardner
Directors ....Mrs. Jefferson McKinley (Chairperson)
         Mrs. Minerva Newport (Assistant)

In an interesting historical note, Du Bois himself (at the age of fifteen) was elected temporary secretary of the Sewing Society on 19 December 1883, when temporary officers were needed for the hour or two between the termination of the existing board and the election of the new board. His biographer, David Levering Lewis, suggests that Du Bois's involvement with the Sewing Society was the beginning of a lifelong pattern of his working closely with women.

The Sewing Society suppers were open to the entire community and were held in members' homes; over the years in the homes of Jason Cooley, Lucinda Gardner, Mrs. J. Moore, William Crosley, Mrs. M. Van Allen, Manuel Mason, and Jefferson McKinley. The suppers often included entertainment (as did weekly meetings, on occasion) and raised money for the church, whose major expense was paying the visiting pastors. Du Bois reported that the entertainment varied:

They were entertained at their last meeting by speaking by the children. And Mr. Egbert Lee related some interesting stories of his experience in the late war.

After the supper there will be a debate on the following question: "Ought the Indian to have been driven out of America?" Messrs. Crosley and Du Bois will take part in the discussion. . . . The debate which I spoke of in my last letter took place last Wednesday evening at the house of Mr. William Crosly [sic]. It was contested warmly on both sides and strong arguments were brought up. It was finally decided in favor of the affirmative.

The last monthly supper of the Zion Sewing Society, at Mrs. L. Gardner's, passed off enjoyably and the company was

entertained by Mr. Fred Sumea, who plays finely upon the
accordion, and by a debate between Messrs. Mason and Chinn
on the well-worn question: "Which is the more destructive, Fire
or Water?" Mr. Chinn on the side of Fire was decided victor.

In May 1883 the Sewing Society formed a Literary Society. As Elizabeth McHenry has recently pointed out in her book on African American literary societies, *Forgotten Readers*, literary societies were a significant component of Black life beginning in the early nineteenth century and continuing well into the twentieth century. As elsewhere, the formation of the Literary Society by the small Black community in Great Barrington shows clearly the importance these individuals placed on reading and learning and the discussion of ideas. Well into the next century the society and other church groups remained active, organizing public readings, plays, musicals, debates, concerts, and guest speakers (including Du Bois himself). Most of these events were public ones, staged in larger venues than that of the church, such as the second-floor meeting room of the town hall (at the time the whole second floor was open for meetings), and the paying public helped support the church.

In February 1884 the church expanded again with the formation of the Children's Mite Society. In an interesting historical twist, what we know of the society is from Du Bois's newspaper columns, and the society was formed by Mrs. Jefferson McKinley, the Sunday school teacher, and with her husband, Jefferson, owner of the building where Du Bois was born. The society's officers were the children themselves:

President .... Francis Mason
Vice President .... Inez Gardner
Secretary .... Walter Mason
Assistant .... George Jackson
Treasurer .... Lulu Jackson

The purpose of the Mite Society was to provide education for the children and to organize performances by the children to raise money for the church building. The educational role of the society and, later, of the Sunday school cannot be overemphasized. Except perhaps for Du Bois, educational opportunity was not equal for Black and white children in Great Barrington. The private schools were open only to whites, and not all Black children attended the public schools. It was not until the 1920s that Black children routinely attended school through high school. The Mite Society and the Sunday school were the primary venues for education in the Black community, and through them the children were taught music, rhetoric, and public speaking, and were introduced to new ideas.

The first performance of the Mite Society, on 20 September 1884, was a tremendous success and was described in detail by Du Bois:

> *Although the weather was at first threatening, it finally cleared off, so that at 3 P.M. the children began to gather at the residence of Mrs. L. Gardner, resplendent in holiday costumes. The afternoon was pleasantly passed until about six o'clock, when a beautiful repast was served to the young masters and misses. In the evening the parents began to arrive, and were treated to a literary and musical program which would have done justice to older heads. The opening was full chorus by the whole society. Then followed recitations by Miss Inez Gardner, Miss Bertha Wooster and Miss Jeanne Sumea, which was [sic] finely delivered. The solos and duets rendered by the Misses Bertha and Florence Wooster, Sumea, and Gardner, were very enjoyable. Master George Jackson also delivered an interesting declamation. Miss Lulu Jackson, who was the organist of the evening, played "Webster's Funeral March," "Lily Waltz" and several other pieces. (Du Bois 1883–1885; 1884 column, 163)*

In 1884 the church was reorganized and incorporated and a new board of trustees appointed. The process evidently began in early August at a business meeting of the society held at the home of Daniel Brown. The meeting continued three weeks later at the home of Manuel Mason and resulted in the president and vice president resigning, a development that led Du Bois to comment, "It is to be hoped that all present difficulties will be amicably settled, and the society will soon be in working order" (Du Bois 1883–1885; 1884 column, 162). On 13 October a new board of trustees was appointed and, in accord with church policy, a new board was again appointed the following year. Du Bois notes that in November Mary Jackson and William Crosley were afforded probationary membership. Whether this is related to the reorganization and resignation of officers is unknown. Crosley, who was a carriage driver on the Hopkins estate, had been active in the society in previous years, with his living quarters over the stable sometimes used for Sewing Society meetings and for Bible study.

Laying the Cornerstone

In August 1886, sixteen years after the women began raising funds, work began on the church building site. Probably to raise funds for the church, on 2 September the trustees sold a portion of the Elm Court land to Charles E. Gorham for $600. A fair and festival held in September brought in $100, a major success for the time. The cornerstone was laid on 6 October. This was a momentous occasion for the church, and was duly noted that week on page 4 of the *Berkshire Courier:*

> *The corner stone of the A. M. E. Zion church, now in process of erection, on Elm street extension, was laid Tuesday morning, quite a number of the members and friends of the Society being present. The exercises were opened with the reading of a selection from Ritual, followed by a fervent prayer by Rev. V. N. Turner, of the M. E. Church. An appropriate selection from the Scriptures was then read by Rev. F. K. Bird, of Bridgeport, Ct., the responses being made by the people. Rev. Joseph G. Smith afterwards read another selection. . . .*

> *The corner stone, bearing the inscription A. M. E. Zion 1886 was then laid at the north east corner of the building. Within it were placed a copy of the church discipline, minutes of the last annual conference of the New England district, Record of the Society, a copy of the Star of Zion, a connectional organ of the Society, published at Salisbury, N.C., and a copy of the* Berkshire Courier.

> *Mr. Smith then stated that all who felt disposed might contribute such amounts as they pleased, the money to go into the hands of the building committee. This offering amounted to $17.56. The hymn "coronation" was then sung after which the benediction was pronounced by the Rev. Mr. Bird.*

Dedicating the Church

By January 1887, with the exception of the interior decorating, the work was largely complete. The building committee was composed of Rev. Joseph G. Smith, trustee Jason Cooley, and Henry Dresser and J. F. Whiting. Whiting served as treasurer, and he and Dresser, both prominent members of the white community, no doubt served as liaison with the contractor, E. R. Lorraine of Canaan, Connecticut, and the builder, John Mambert of Hudson, New York.

The near-completion of the building in January 1887 brought a front-page story in the *Berkshire Courier* on 12 January:

On Elm street extension, or Elm-place, is now in process of erection a building, where the African M. E. Zion Society, of this village, will hereafter meet to worship. The dimensions of the edifice are 55 x 24 feet, the ceiling being fifteen and one-half feet in the clear, with a truss roof, three trusses being used. The gables are shingled in an ornamental manner. At the north-east corner is a tower, thirty feet in height. Space has been left for a bell whenever one shall have been obtained.

Under the tower is a vestibule, seven feet in diameter[;] a door at the left leads to the body of the church. This room is thirty-nine feet deep by twenty-four feet wide. On either side are four windows, of cathedral glass, the upper half being stained and composed of sixteen small panes, the lower portion consisting of but two large panes. Directly in front is a large double window, similarly finished and over it is a semi-circular stained glass window.

The walls are wainscoted, to a height of three feet, the remainder being hard finished and is to be painted and frescoed.

The pulpit is of ash, and placed upon a rostrum, in the rear of which is a shallow alcove. To the left of this is a platform, seven feet square and elevated eighteen inches, for the accommodation of the choir and organ.

In the rear is a vestry, a pleasant room 22 × 16 feet being the dimensions; this is lighted by three stained glass windows, and has an entrance to itself.

The church is heated by a furnace in the cellar, a large register being in the center of the floor. Twenty pews, built of white wood, will serve to accommodate the congregation. One aisle will run through the center of the room.

Ground was broken for the building early in August of last year. The corner-stone was laid October 6th, and with the exception of the painting, carpeting, etc., the building is completed.

The building, when completed, will have cost about $2,000, and the society is to be congratulated that its earnest efforts, in procuring a permanent home in which to hold its services, has been successful.

The new church was dedicated on 6 February 1887. The ceremony was heavily attended:

*The cosy little church was filled to overflowing by a congregation of the members and their friends of other religious denominations of the vicinity. Many were unable to obtain seats even after a double line of chairs had been placed in the aisles. (*Berkshire Courier *9 February 1887, 4)*

The service was conducted by the church's pastor, Rev. J. G. Smith—with V. N. Traver, the Great Barrington Methodist minister; Rev. William H. Abbott and Rev. F. K. Bird of the A. M. E. Zion churches in New Haven and Bridgeport; and Rev. T. G. Campbell of the A. M. E. Church in Lee—on the podium. The program was as follows:

Introduction and Reading
   of Dedicatory Selections .... Rev. Smith
Reading of Hymn 974:
   "Great King of Glory Come" .... Rev. Abbott

Singing of Hymn 974:

"Great King of Glory Come" .... Quartette Choir and
.... Congregation
Prayer .... Rev. Campbell
First Lesson... Rev. Bird
Second Lesson.. Rev. Campbell
Reading of Hymn 971:

"Thou Who on the Whirlwind Rideth" ...... Rev. Traver
Dedicatory Sermon.................................... Rev. Abbott
Remarks.. Rev. Traver
Collection
Reading of Psalms...................................... Rev. Bird
Presentation of Church for Dedication......... Manuel F. Mason
Dedication .... Rev. Abbott
Thank You and Acknowledgement of Gifts .. Rev. Smith
Signing of the Doxology
Benediction .... Rev. Smith

The *Courier* described and quoted from Reverend Abbott's dedicatory sermon at length:

The Pastor then introduced the Rev. William H. Abbott as having been selected to preach the dedicatory sermon. Mr. Abbott had selected for his text the 41st and 42nd verses of the 6th chapter of II Chronicles. The sermon, which was extemporaneous, was an earnest, practical exposition of the important duties belonging to the relation of the people towards their master, their church and their pastor. "We have the presence of God in our midst," said Mr. Abbott, "for He has said wherever my name is recorded, lo, I will be there." "Here you have a beautiful church, erected to the glory of God, through the kindness of friends and the efforts of your pastor and yourselves," continued the speaker, "but if God does not abide here it will only be a decorated folly."

"Israel did not hear from God for 400 years. How terrible that was, yet we have churches in our midst in which the master is

*not present—where from one year to another we never hear
of a conversion. Why is this? Because God has withdrawn his
presence from them." Mr. Abbott then went on to state that
the Methodist Church especially the branch to which the one
in question belongs, has been a power among the nations in
times past. He wished to say to the colored clergy and their
people, that they must be educated; not only that, we must have
the power—the presence of the Christ—in our midst, else this
edifice will not accomplish the work for which it was designed.*

*"These walls," said Mr. Abbott, "we erect and consecrate and
dedicate to the service of God. It is not the place we are to
worship, but it is the Being who makes the place sacred. What
would this church be without his presence? Only a decorated
folly. Let us not forget that it is the Master . . . we seek in the
gathering of his people. No matter who may administer from the
holy desk. Come, and go away glad."*

*"Some come to church to see and to be seen," continued the
speaker, "some to admire and be admired, but the Christian
comes to worship God." Later on he stated, "[A]s rivers and
streams mingle together in the boundless ocean, so we the
Presbyterians, the Congregationalists, the Episcopalians, the
Methodists all are journeying to one home. When you sin,
said St. James, sin with a spirit; when you pray, pray with a
spirit. Don't make your church a sad, gloomy place. Leave your
sorrows outside. If you want to make Brother Smith eloquent,
and he can be eloquent, let him see the light of God shining in
your eyes. You can make your pastor as dry as mouldy bread,
or make him eloquent by having the love of God in your hearts.
Be in harmony with him, love him, and let there be no confusion
among you."*

*"If you don't love your pastor you can't go to heaven, though you
say you do love Jesus," he exclaimed emphatically. Mr. Abbott
wished that side-shows, theatricals and fairs which desecrate the
house of God could be abolished and the place kept sacred. He*

*concluded with a prayer for the success of the church in which they were assembled. (*Berkshire Courier *9 February 1887, 4)*

The new church benefited from several gifts from members of the Great Barrington community:

Organ from Clark W. Bryan
Bible from F. T. Whiting
Desk covering from Mrs. J. A. Bryan
Bookmark from Miss M. A. Whiting
Chair from Mrs. Charles Benton
Bible from the Congregational Society
Music stool from E. B. Culver and Manuel F. Mason
Book racks from E. R. Lorraine

In offering thanks for the gifts, Reverend Smith noted:

*We have friends, he said, and if we do our duty God will keep our friends by us. To you that have been so kind to us, I think I express the wishes of our society when I say may God guide you in his footsteps and fill your hearts with his grace and keep your pockets full as well, and let us be ready and willing to help others as we have been helped. (*Berkshire Courier *9 February 1887, 4)*

The land, church, and interior cost $4,275:

Land $1,500
Foundation $275
Building $2,100
Heating $150
Carpets, Furniture,
Lighting $175
Incidentals $75

The church had raised $2,600 through the sale of the south Main Street plot, sale of a portion the Elm Court land, and a $1,000 mortgage secured on 3 February 1887 from the Great Barrington Savings Bank. The additional funds were raised through donations and church activities.

The first regular worship service was held on 11 February, and the women of the church went to work again to raise the funds to retire the debt. They held a supper in April, an ice cream festival in May, the annual strawberry festival in June, a "blue sociable" in July, the first annual fair and festival in August, an oyster supper in November, a Sunday school concert in December, and the major event, a grand rally, in December:

> On the fourth Sunday of this month [December], the 25th
> instant, there will be a Grand Rally in the A. M. E. Zion church
> for the purpose of lifting the mortgage of $1,000 on the church.
> The Clinton Battalion and auxiliary, composed of members
> of the church, [have] been divided into ten companies, and
> are now out skirmishing in order to capture funds for the
> above purpose, and they solicit all lovers of evangelization,
> Christianity and civilization to help them. On the above date
> there will be present, to preach at each service, eminent
> clergymen from New York and Connecticut. (Berkshire Courier
> 14 December 1887, 4).

Growth and Some Troubles

If building and dedicating the church were not enough, 1887 also saw the arrival of a new pastor. Reverend Joseph G. Smith, who had so ably guided the society through the building process, was reassigned to New Bedford, Massachusetts, very likely a promotion to a larger church, and was replaced by Rev. George H. Simmons from Attleboro, Massachusetts. Simmons was to prove himself an unfortunate selection.

With a permanent home in the center of town, the church became a more visible presence in the Great Barrington religious community. Church services were now regularly listed alongside those of the other churches in the weekly *Courier*, and greater effort, following on the work of the Clinton Battalion, was made to raise money to pay off the mortgage. The first major event was the first annual anniversary service, held on 5 February, with a turkey supper the following day. On

17 February there was a donation party at Reverend Simmons's home, "leaving the pastor more blessed in this world's goods to the extent of twenty dollars in cash, and groceries, provisions, and kindred articles to the value of thirteen dollars" *(Berkshire Courier* 22 February 1888, 4). The remainder of the year saw the usual schedule of suppers and socials, but some new activities as well, including a children's day in July and a lawn-party benefit at Jason Cooley's home on East Street in August.

During 1888 the church also began to become more involved with the A. M. E. Zion denomination. In January Reverend Simmons attended the Allegheny Conference of the church in Pittsburgh. April was perhaps the highlight of the year, with page 4 of the *Berkshire Courier* announcing that

> *the Rt. Rev. J. W. Hood, D. D., Bishop of the 1st Episcopal*
> *District of the A. M. E. Zion church will lecture in Town Hall,*
> *on the subject, The Negro Church, Thursday evening, April 5,*
> *1888, at 7:30 p.m. . . . The Bishop will preach in the A. M. E.*
> *Zion church, on Friday evening, April 6th, after which he will be*
> *tendered a reception in the vestry.*

Bishop Hood (1831–1918) was a major figure in the church and at the time was stationed in Fayetteville, North Carolina. He developed the church in North Carolina, helped found the *Star of Zion* (the denomination's newspaper), was the first African American clergyman to compile a book of sermons (*The Negro in the Christian Pulpit*), and in 1895 wrote what is still considered an authoritative church history (*One Hundred Years of the African Methodist Episcopal Zion Church*). Hood Theological Seminary is named in his honor. Whether Hood actually deliveredhis lecture or not is unclear, since the *Courier* provides no follow-up to the announcement.

Three other notable events in the church's history took place in 1888. On 26 May, at the Quarterly Conference, Manuel Mason resigned as a member of the church and gave up his official duties. Because Mason had been a founder of the church, served on the trustee and building committees, was a strong supporter of the Sunday school, and was well respected in the Great Barrington community, his resignation must have been a serious loss to the church. History tells us nothing about why or the circumstances of his resignation. On 16 July the women organized a Parish Aid Society, which was to play a major role in future fund-raising and which enhanced the status of women in the church. Finally, in November, Reverend Simmons was arrested for threatening his wife and fled town. The *Courier's* page 4 reporting of the incident on 14 November was uncharacteristically harsh:

> *Rev. George H. Simmons, the colored pastor, who was brought before the District Court last week for threatening his wife, left town yesterday afternoon. It is hoped our colored brethren will be more careful hereafter in the selection of their clergymen and that they will without delay restore Mr. and Mrs. Manuel Mason to church membership.*

In reality, the church membership was not responsible for the pastor, since they had little influence in selecting the pastor assigned to their church. Simmons's departure left the church without pastoral leadership and disrupted the service schedule until a new pastor arrived in February 1889.

The final year of the decade began on a low note, with the church without a pastor, without the leadership of Manuel Mason, and with pressing bills totaling $200 in addition to the unpaid mortgage. A waffle supper on 18 January, followed by a rally (a fund-raising event) on 20 January, produced a profit of $41. In February the Mason family moved into their new home, an event covered on page 4 of the 13 February issue of the *Berkshire Courier*. The coverage suggests that Mason continued to enjoy considerable prestige in town:

> *Mr. Manuel Mason and family have recently moved into their new home, on the road leading to reservoir. It is a neat and attractive house of two and a half stories, with parlor, hall, dining-room, and kitchen on the first floor, and above are three chambers and a large attic. The house has all the modern conveniences in the way of furnace, water, sewage, etc. It has a healthy location and commands a fine view of the valley.*

*Last Thursday a "house warming" was given Mr. and Mrs.
Mason, from 4 to 10 o'clock, and a large number of friends
testified their regard for the honest and industrious couple by
nearly furnishing their new home, bringing a parlor set, rugs,
curtains, lambrequins, vases, books, albums, stands, clothes,
pictures, lamps, cut glass, silver, etc. Mr. and Mrs. Mason
entertained all with a bountiful supper.*

Unfortunately, the Mason family was struck by tragedy only a few weeks later, when the Masons' sixteen-year-old son Walter, a founding member of the Mite Society and a high school student, died at home on 25 March. The Masons rejoined the church, and in June Manuel Mason was appointed superintendent of the Sunday school.

Revival Under Reverend Waters

In late February of 1889, regular church services resumed under the direction of Rev. John H. Waters, with prayer meetings held each Thursday evening as well. At the New England Conference in Worcester in May, Reverend Waters was appointed pastor and Reverend Simmons, who had disgraced himself and the church the previous November, was expelled from the ministry. The first half of the year was especially busy with meetings of the Literary Club, and the Aid Society now added to the usual schedule of socials and suppers. In June the first quarterly meeting was held under the direction of Rev. S. J. McCutcheon, and the Children's Day events were a great success, with a speech by Manuel Mason. The *Courier* reported that a "declamation, recitations and solos were well rendered by the scholars. A quartette of Miss Emma Mason, Mrs. J. H. Waters, Mr. M. Mason, Sr. and J. F. Waters was one of the features of the programme" (*Berkshire Courier* 26 June 1889, 4).

By July the unfortunate events of 1888 had been put behind them, and the trustees placed an announcement in the *Courier* informing the town of the church's success:

*The rally of the A. M. E. Zion church last Sabbath was a
grand success, the sum of $62.87 being raised. The young
and energetic pastor, Rev. J. F. Waters, is far ahead of his*

> predecessors. *It will be remembered that Mr. Waters was*
> *appointed to this charge at a critical period, when the church*
> *was divided and no services had been held from October till*
> *February 23rd. The church is now in a flourishing condition,*
> *having a Sabbath school, a literary society, two associations,*
> *and as fine a choir as can be found in the county. The feature of*
> *this rally is that the colored citizens, though small in number,*
> *gave $43.75 of the $62.87. Let the colored citizens of Great*
> *Barrington rally around the young and earnest pastor and*
> *thereby show their appreciation. Rev. Samuel Harrison of*
> *Pittsfield and Rev. F. R. Marvin of Great Barrington officiated at*
> *the services last Sabbath.* (Berkshire Courier *17 July 1889, 4)*

The year and the first two decades of the small church's life concluded with a series of happy events. In July Du Bois returned to town with a Harvard classmate, Clement G. Morgan, to give a series of readings under the auspices of the Congregational Church. On 31 July the *Courier* reported on page 4 that "the young gentlemen showed evidence of careful and thorough drill, and every piece was applauded by the audience." In August Reverend Waters presented "A Light from the Lighthouse," which was so well received that he presented it a second time in October. And, on Thanksgiving, the church presented a union service with the Congregational and Methodist churches. The Methodist minister, Rev. S. J. McCutcheon, presided, and singing and responsive reading was led by the Clinton Sunday school students.

W. E. B. Du Bois and the Clinton Church

An interesting question raised by the research for this history is just what relationship and ties W. E. B. Du Bois had to the Zion Society and the Clinton Church. Answering this question is difficult due to the paucity of historical source material about the church for the 1870s and 1880s, the time period during which Du Bois was growing up in Great Barrington. The best information we have about the church for this period comes from Du Bois himself—the thirty columns he wrote for the *New York Globe* from 1883 to 1885. Each column describes life in the community for the previous one or two months.

Du Bois and the Clinton Church came of age over the same period of years. Du Bois was born in 1868, and the A. M. E. Zion Society was formed in Great Barrington no later than 1870 and more likely a few years earlier. Du Bois graduated from high school in 1884, the same year the church incorporated as a fully organized A. M. E. Zion church. As Du Bois grew up, so, too, did the church, as it became the center of Black community in Great Barrington. Throughout Du Bois's childhood and youth, many members of the Black community in the southern Berkshires were active in the church. Black membership in the white churches, which had always been minimal, ceased almost entirely.

In his many writings later in his career about the Black church, African American life, and religion, Du Bois makes little mention of the Clinton Church or his involvement in it, although many of his conclusions about the Black church in American life—the centrality of the church in community life, the contributions of women, the unique contribution of Black church music—were things he first witnessed or experienced as a youth in Great Barrington while attending A. M. E. Zion Society events.

The little mention he makes of the Zion Society in his scholarly writings provides an odd contrast to the ample attention he gives the Society in his articles for the *New York Globe*. In these dispatches he mentions the Zion Society and its activities regularly and at length. He could not have done otherwise, as the Zion Society was the central institution in Black Great Barrington. Many of the Black residents were members, and most attended at least some events. In 1903 when he wrote the following in his *The Souls of Black Folk*, he could have been and perhaps was describing the Clinton Church of his boyhood as well as many other Black churches:

The Negro church of to-day is the social center of Negro life in the United States, and the most characteristic expression of African character. . . . Thus one can see in the Negro church to-day, reproduced in microcosm, all the great world from which the Negro is cut off by color-prejudice and social condition.

It is clear from these early writings that he had regular involvement with the Zion Society, attended prayer meetings, participated in meetings of the Sewing and Literary Society, and regularly interacted with members of the church. It is impossible to say if he was a "member," as no membership rolls survive from those years. But, since he was elected temporary secretary of the Zion Sewing Society in 1883 and clearly attended the key business meeting in 1884 when the church was reorganized, it seems reasonable to conclude that he was viewed by others as a member. In one of his columns he went so far as to comment that he hoped that the current conflict among trustees of the church would be soon resolved.

Du Bois was also in daily contact with others who were active in the church. Despite his claim that the church was formed by "newcomers" and disapproved of by old families, the record tells us otherwise. Some members of these old families were among the church's early members, including several of his Burghardt kin, such as the Woosters, Newports, Freemans, and Pipers. The church was founded by a mix of longtime residents and recent arrivals from the South. Du Bois was of the former group but also friendly with people in the latter. For example, in his *Autobiography,* Du Bois mentions his fondness for the Mason family. He is referring to Manuel and Emily Mason and their children. Du Bois noted that they were very religious, and they were one the founding families of the church and the Sunday school as well as active members for over twenty-five years.

Du Bois's family, the Burghardts, were so involved in the church that in 1880 the pastor, Silas Mitchell, boarded in Du Bois's uncle's house on the Burghardt farm with Du Bois's cousin, Lucinda Wooster. On return visits to town after 1885, Du Bois himself stayed with relatives who were trustees of the church, including Lucinda Wooster and the Burget family. In 1894 he was the featured speaker at the annual church fund-raising event, for which he delivered a talk, "Some Impressions of Europe." The *Berkshire Courier* reported on the event and noted that his talk was well attended and favorably received.

As David Levering Lewis points out, Du Bois knew more about Black culture outside New England before heading South in 1885 than he later claimed. This knowledge came though involvement with the Zion Society and its members, some of whom had recently arrived from the South.

After leaving Great Barrington in 1885, Du Bois maintained regular contact with relatives and friends in Great Barrington. Over the next fifteen years, he came back to visit several times and more than a dozen articles or announcements in the weekly *Courier* reported on his latest publications, travels, and academic postings. His daughter was born in Great Barrington and attended school there, and he chose to bury his infant son in Mahaiwe Cemetery. To what extent they were involved with the Clinton Church is unknown, but they were in regular contact with Burghardt relatives who were members.

How do we explain this contradiction between his claimed and actual involvement with the Zion Society? There are a few possible explanations. One is that Du Bois moved easily across the color line in Great Barrington and this pattern applied as well to his association with the Black and white religious institutions. Clearly, his involvement with the First Congregational Church had more to offer him in terms of life opportunities, such as the education afforded by the Sunday school, contact with leading white citizens, and financial support for college. At the same time, as a son of the Black community, he had strong relationships with members of that community and an identification with the community that would have involved him in the church and its activities. His writings suggest that his participation was social and intellectual, not spiritual.

A second explanation is that Du Bois, even as a teenager, was much concerned about the lack of political involvement by Blacks and, as he wrote later, may have already seen the church as an agent of the existing order rather than an agent of political transformation. If this was the case, it is easy to understand why he could report at length about the church's activities but not consider those activities especially significant to his life.

A third and final explanation is that Du Bois, again from a young age, saw himself as an intellectual and researcher first. Along with most other intellectuals of the time, he saw religious belief and knowledge arrived at through research as quite distinct. If this was the case, his early religious experiences would not have seemed a major influence on his life.

CHAPTER 3

Growth and Decline

The 1890s began where the 1880s left off—with a *Berkshire Courier* column on 1 January reporting on a sermon by Rev. John Waters delivered in late December 1889. The reverend argued in favor of building an expensive casino (public meeting hall) that could be used for religious services. He further argued that it was the duty of clergy both to speak out against actions that would harm the community and to register support of those "tending to advance the moral status of our community," such as the casino. The *Courier* editorialized that "the willingness of this enterprising young pastor to come out so boldly and make so decided a stand for what he believes to be for the advantage of the community, is certainly to be commended." This event was remarkable for the times both because Reverend Waters spoke out forcefully on a public issue and because his opinion was welcomed by the newspaper.

In February the Clinton Church was again the center of community attention when it hosted a New England supper at the GAR (Grand Army of the Republic) Hall. The event drew over 400 people who voted on the winner, which was Jason Cooley, who won a gold-headed cane. A social success, the event raised a substantial sum for the church. Raising money remained a pressing matter for the church, since it still owed $1,000 on the mortgage and another $200 in debt had accumulated on operating expenses. The major operating expense was paying and housing the pastor.

Also in February the church celebrated its third anniversary with a full day of events on Sunday the 15th. Mrs. Jefferson McKinley presented a history of the church, and Manuel Mason a progress report.

The afternoon service was conducted by the Methodist minister, Rev. S. J. McCutcheon and his choir, with readings by Clinton members Miss H. F. Mason, Miss L. Freeman, Clara Gunn, and Miss C. Ferris, and a sermon by Rev. Waters. The evening was given over to musical performances by the Zion choir, Rev. Waters, and solo musicians from the community. According to the *Courier* (19 February 1890, 1), "at the evening exercises the audience present was the largest in the history of the church. Even the standing room was crowded to the door and the little chapel likewise filled."

With the Black community now numbering about 120 and a very active pastor in Rev. Waters, the Clinton Church was a beehive of activity. Postings in the *Courier* listed the following weekly activities:

Monday evening ..... Literary Association
Wednesday evening Willing Workers
Thursday evening ... Prayer and Praise
Sunday
10:30 a.m. .... Preaching
11:30 a.m. .... Class
12:00 p.m. .... Sunday school
6:00 p.m. .... Clinton Lyceum
7:30 p.m. .... Preaching

In addition, there were suppers each month, usually on a Friday evening, given by the women of the church to raise money. Depending on the meal, the charge ranged from ten to thirty-five cents.

Another important source of funds and community involvement were public performances put on by church members. In February the church Sunday school hosted a literary contest, with Manuel Mason Jr. taking the essay prize for his "Gifts" and Clara Gunn taking the recitation prize for her "Comfort." Other contestants were Miss H. F. Mason, Lulu Jackson, and Cora Ferris (*Berkshire Courier* 5 February 1890, 4). In April the church benefited from a performance of Theodore Thomas's "The Picnic," and on 9 July members staged a performance of "A Feast in the Wilderness" at the town hall. The latter performance was evidently unique in its complexity and was described in the *Courier* (25 June 1890, 4) as follows:

It is entitled "A Feast in the Wilderness" and will be illustrative of scenes and incidents in the life of the Israelites, from the time of their leaving their country until the cross of the Red sea. The programme will comprise tableaux, dialogues, jubilee singing, etc. and the proceeds will be for the benefit of the church.

The Departure of Pastor Waters

Both the church and Great Barrington suffered a loss in May when Rev. Waters was reassigned by the New England Conference to a larger church in Norwich, Massachusetts. In anticipation of his departure, Rev. Waters delivered a farewell sermon in which he reviewed the state of the church. He noted that there were now 126 Black people in town and that the church in the past year had raised $681.15, and had seen two marriages and two deaths among its members. He thanked the church members, townsfolk, and the *Courier* for the support they had given him. In appreciation of his efforts, the church and town awarded him with a gift of $75 and provisions, and the *Courier* (7 May 1890, 4) called attention to his contribution: "Rev. Mr. Waters on his arrival found the church disorganized, deeply in debt and in a low state generally, but he has worked hard and faithfully and his efforts have been rewarded with very encouraging success." Moreover, the *Courier* continued to monitor his career, noting that he was enjoying success at Norwich and the following year promoted to a larger congregation in Worcester, Massachusetts. James Hood's church history (1895) indicates that by then Waters had been promoted to elder in the New England Conference.

Replacing Reverend Waters was Rev. G. A. Given, who devoted himself to the spiritual needs of the church. In June he organized a Love Feast, in July presented a sermon titled "The Duties of Parents," and in August hosted a lecture, "Lucifer: Son of the Morning," by his brother, Rev. Joseph V. Given. Unfortunately, Rev. G. A. Given took ill and had to resign his position. In December the church and other members of the Great Barrington community organized a concert to raise money for enabling him to return to the South to rest and regain his health.

Without a pastor, church activities slowed in 1891, although several suppers and a musical performance in March were organized. In June the New England Conference appointed S. W. Hutchings pastor. The musical performances of the church were popular in town, and a concert in August was remarked on in the *Courier* (20 August 1891, 4):

> *The Sunday School of Zion church gave a concert Sunday night, a very pleasing programme of songs being rendered. The church has a number of excellent singers now and their music is not surpassed, if equaled, by the larger churches.*

Retiring the Debt

In 1892 Reverend Hutchings took a more aggressive approach to reducing the church's debt when he announced in October that a "subscription paper" would be circulated in town "with the idea of raising funds to pay off the mortgage on the Zion church property" (*Berkshire Courier* 13 October 1892, 4). The project proved a success, with the debt of $1,000 reduced to $800 by early November, $560 by early December, and $498 by the end of the year.

The reverend's efforts were noted by the *Courier* on 6 April 1893, when it opined that it hoped that the New England Conference would keep him on at the Clinton Church. But, as was its practice, the Conference replaced Reverend Hutchings with Rev. Alfred Day in May. Reverend Day had in the 1880s been one of three "auditors" of the Book Concern of the central church. In July the trustees of the church continued the communitywide fund-raising activity with the following report in the *Courier* (20 July 1893, 8):

> *Zion M. E. Church*
> *Report of the Trustees of the Colored Church.*
>
> *By the generous gifts of the many benevolent friends who aided us the past year, the mortgage debt has been reduced from $1,000 to the present amount of $465. Very little reduction has been made on the floating indebtedness, which now is near $200—making a total of $665, which the trustees are anxious to pay, and pray the Lord will open up many kind hearts to help them.*
>
> *We must have a minister and it taxes us to our utmost to provide for him in the most economical manner possible.*

We have arranged to limit the pastor's salary—including incidental expenses, board of pastor, and running expenses of the church for the ensuing year—to $475. We shall be thankful for any help, be it ever so small.

Seats are free to all. Preaching Sunday morning at 11 A.M. Sunday school at 12 P.M. Preaching at 8 P.M., and prayer meeting on Thursday evening.

You who are stewards of God, do not forget the little colored church of Great Barrington, Mass.

We have appointed the following stewardesses, to whom contributions can be given for the pastor's fund: Sisters Margaret McKinley, Maria Burget, Laura Suma, Jennie Moore, Emily Mason, Sarah Ferris and Lucinda Wooster. [On 4 August the Courier *reported that Mrs. Inez Freeman and Mrs. Minerva Newport were also stewardesses.]*

We desire to express our heartfelt thanks to the citizens of Great Barrington and all others who have aided us in the past, and hope we may prove worthy of your beneficence.

Yours in the interest of truth, morality and the Church of Christ.

> E. Mason, Pres't.
> Jason Cooley, Sec'y.
> Pastor, Rev. A. Day. Post-office box 709.

Beyond this public appeal, fund-raising continued to be the work of the women of the church, through the monthly dime suppers, a Japanese tea hosted by the Sewing Society in December, and a fair in September that produced $100.

During the year the *Courier* (6 April, 4) continued its practice of covering the activities of prominent members of the Black community in its "Local News and Notes" column when it reported that Manuel Mason had "renovated and repaired" his new restaurant on Railroad Street. In July

Ads for Jason Cooley's and Manuel Mason's eating establishments placed in the *Southern Berkshire Directory* in the 1890s.

it noted that a fire on the roof of the building had caused minimal damage and in August that Mrs. Mason and three of her children had gotten into an altercation with police officer McCormick, resulting in fines of $10 for John Mason and $1 each for his sisters Francis and Emily.

The year of 1894 was marked by several significant events at the church. The members staged several productions to raise funds and provide entertainment for the Great Barrington community. In May they presented the musical "The Crowning of the Queen," which was well received: "Great credit is due those who managed and those who took part, and another presentation of the same character would doubtless attract a large audience" *(Berskhire Courier* 10 May 1894, 4). This success was followed by a Children's Sunday "Day of Song and Flowers" to raise money for the A. M. E. Zion's Livingstone College in Salisbury, North Carolina, and then a fair and festival on 28–29 August, including a performance of the cantata "A Quarrel among the Flowers."

Another major fund-raising event took place on 25 July, when W. E. B. Du Bois delivered a talk entitled "Some Impressions of Europe." The *Courier* (26 July 1894, 4) noted: "Mr. Du Bois' remarks were very interesting and a good sized audience greeted the speaker. An excellent supper was served, and a neat sum netted for the church." Du Bois had also been in Great Barrington in June, staying with the family of Maria Burget, a church stewardess, and perhaps it was during that visit that he was asked to participate in the fund-raising evening. Several drafts of Du Bois's handwritten text of the speech are in the Du Bois Collection at the University of Massachusetts, and copies of the microfilm edition of his opening remarks and his description of the Rhine River follow.

The last major entertainment event of the year took place on 20 September and was afforded a detailed announcement in the *Courier* (13 September 1894, 4):

> *GRAND MUSICAL TREAT*
> *In the A. M. E. Zion church, Thursday evening, Sept. 20th,*
> *"Little Bessie, the human singing bird," and J. H. Manley,*
> *missionary secretary of Zion connection," will discourse [on]*
> *some of their choice melodies. They will be assisted by "Blind*
> *Tom, No. 2," accompanist who will also render some of his*
> *favorite selections."*

Reverend Hatfield and His Illustrated Sermons

In May 1894 the New England Conference appointed Rev. Chauncey Hatfield the new pastor, and in December the church staged a fund-raiser for the benefit of the pastor and his two children. He was a widower, who later remarried, to June Bell of Philadelphia in June 1895. In January 1895 Reverend Hatfield offered what the *Courier* (17 January, 4) described as a "picture sermon": "The sermon will be beautifully illustrated by stereopticon views." An optical device, the stereopticon is used to enlarge and view images, sometimes seemingly in three dimensions, on cards; it was a popular form of home entertainment in the 1890s. Hatfield earned a living producing lantern transparencies, and also as a photographer.

The pastor's "illustrated sermons" proved popular, and in February he used the chalkboard and the stereopticon to illustrate talks before the Sabbath school and in his sermons entitled "The Temple of God" and "God's Protection over His People" as well as in an Easter sermon, "Christ Victorious over Death and the Grave." The illustration highlight of the year took place on 20 March:

A page of text written by W. E. B. Du Bois for his talk at the church in 1894.
Source: W. E. B. Du Bois Collection, University of Massachusetts, Amherst.

> *On Wednesday evening March 20, something new under the sun*
> *will be shown. Rev. Mr. Hatfield has succeeded in constructing*
> *an instrument that will magnify solid objects. The instrument*
> *will be exhibited in Zion Church on the above date. One of the*
> *features of the entertainment will be the exhibition of portraits.*
> *All who attend the entertainment has the privilege of bringing*
> *a portrait of their friend which he will be pleased to exhibit on*
> *the screen life size. Admission 15 cents.* (Berkshire Courier *14*
> *March, 1895, 4)*

The exact nature of Reverend Hatfield's projector is unknown, but it likely combined features of the stereopticon with those of early film projectors that took their light from a firebox. Tragically, the device caused the pastor's death the following April (1896):

> *At the time of the accident the injuries did not appear so serious*
> *as they subsequently turned out to be. The burns around the*
> *neck, a celluloid collar which he wore taking fire, were very*
> *deep, the head was badly burned and one ear burned almost to*
> *a crisp. The hands and arms were burned, but not as bad as the*
> *other portions. The nervous shock, however, was so severe, that*
> *it was undoubtedly the cause of his death.* (Berkshire Courier
> *16 April 1896, 1)*

Reverend Hatfield died on the 16th and was buried in New Haven, Connecticut, the city of his youth, following a service at the United Methodist Church in Great Barrington conducted by the town's clergy.

The Sunday School Convention

The major event of 1895 was the annual convention of the Sunday Schools of the New England Conference of the A. M. E. Zion Church, held at the Clinton Church during the first week of September. Drawing several dozen pastors and teachers, the event was of sufficient local importance that it garnered first-page coverage in the *Courier*. The out-of-town participants included the following:

Rev. F. S. Dickson .... New Haven, CT
Rev. W. B. Bowens .... Ansonia, CT
Rev. W. B. Fenderson ..... Cambridgeport, MA
Rev. S. C. Birchmore .... Providence, RI
Rev. G. H. S. Bell .... Waterbury, CT
Rev. F. H. Hill .... Providence, RI
Rev. D. C. Holbrook .... New Yorkn NY
Rev. L. H. Taylor .... Hartford, CT
Rev. William Brown .... New Haven, CT
Rev. C. C. Ringgold .... Willimantic, CT
C. A. C. Beaman .... Middletown, CT
Mrs. G. H. S. Bell .... Waterbury, CT
Miss L. Ziegler .... Norwich, CT
Miss E. H. Miner .... Boston, MA
Miss Gertrude Day .... Waterbury, CT
George E Ruffian .... Boston, MA
Samuel Jameson .... Boston, MA
Jacob W. Powell .... Boston, MA

Welcoming remarks were offered by Manual Mason Jr., and the convention heard reports on Sunday school attendance and discussed educational literature and the problem of keeping boys in Sunday school. The committee on the state of the nation issued a report expressing grave concern about the treatment of Black people and about lynching. There were nearly 5,000 lynchings in the United States from 1882 to 1968. About 80 percent took place in the South, and 73 percent of those lynched were Black. Whites who were lynched were typically accused of helping Blacks or of opposing lynching. The committee noted:

> *Although there is reported to be a revival of industry throughout*
> *the land, and this year's grain crop is tremendous in its*
> *proportions, the condition of the Negro citizen in this nation*
> *continues to be one of anxious solitude. The deplorable spirit*
> *of lawlessness, as manifested in lynchings, seems no longer*
> *to continue itself within its former well understood limits,*
> *but, while still controlling action in its old familiar haunts,*
> *is spreading itself over the land, entering even that splendid*

*commonwealth, which gave to our nation the immortal
president, Abraham Lincoln. What we need in this critical
condition of public affairs is just what we needed in the dark
days of slavery—men to "stand on the wall." As did Garrison,
Phillips, Sumner and Douglas[s], hurling their thunderbolts
at the citadel of injustice, and swaying the rulers and people
of the American nation into a recognition and practice of the
principles of the constitution of the United States. God's blessing
cannot long continue with a nation whose people are indifferent
to, or careless of the claims of justice to each and all of its
citizens. The future of our country depends upon our activity
along the lines laid down in the great command, "Thou shalt
love the Lord thy God with all thy heart; and thy neighbor as
thyself"* (Berkshire Courier *5 September 1895, 1*).

The conference concluded on Friday with an evening of musical and literary entertainment.

The *Great Barrington Directory* for 1894–1895 listed the following Clinton Church officers:

Pastor	Alfred Day
Trustees	M. F. Mason
	Jason Cooley
	George Harding
	A. Williams
Preacher steward	M. F. Mason
Treasurer	G. Harding
Clerk	Jason Cooley
Sunday school superintendent	M. F. Mason
Secretary	Miss Emma Mason
Organist	Miss Francis Mason
Church Aid Society	Mrs. James Burghardt (President)
	Mrs. D. M. Jackson (Secretary)
	Mrs. D. Brown (Treasurer)

Manuel Mason and Jason Cooley

As noted in chapter one, Manuel Mason and Jason Cooley, two of the leading men of the Black community and also respected in the white community, were among the leaders of the church for many years. Mason served as president and Sunday school superintendent and Cooley as clerk, trustee, and as a member of the Building Committee. Both also opened their homes for church and community events. The first half of the 1890s comprised evidently good years for the two men and their families. Both were entrepreneurs. Mason derived his income from his catering and restaurant, which was located on Railroad Street. Cooley also ran a restaurant, located in the Hollister block on the corner of Main and Bridge streets, which he relocated to Main Street in October 1896. Both men placed ads in the 1894–1895 regional directory, which are reproduced on page 52. Mason's building was destroyed in the October 1896 Railroad Street fire. He estimated his loss at $1,600 and said he was insured for only $1,100. He chose not to rebuild and instead relocated to Springfield with his family. In 1900 he sold off the last of his property in Great Barrington.

Cooley was employed as a janitor by the school system as well, earning $228 in 1894–1895, $265 in 1895–1896, and $87 in 1896–1897. His employment by the town government was unusual, since government jobs were given almost exclusively to whites. The town assessor's report for 1894 indicates that Cooley was quite well-off, his personal property assessed at $170, one building at $1,200, a second building at $900, and 1 acre of land at $400. His total tax of $28.70 placed him in the top 20 percent of taxpayers, although considerably below the richest men in town, whose annual tax bills ran to over $100. In 1899 he was listed in the *Courier* as one of the largest taxpayers, with a bill now of $30.90. Mason also owned property, with his personal property assessed at $50, a building at $800, and a half-acre of land at $200. His total tax was $12.50 for 1894.

Presiding Elder Nathaniel J. Greene

In 1895 Rev. Nathaniel J. Greene, presiding elder of the New England Conference, died. As presiding elder he had led the Quarterly Conferences at

Presiding Elder Nathaniel Greene.

the Clinton Church for several years and advised on pastor changes as well as on fund-raising initiatives. Reverend Greene was a highly respected officer of the church and was profiled in Hood's 1895 centennial.

Elder Greene was born in Philadelphia on 6 August 1849 and educated in local schools. In 1864 he joined the navy and served for three years on several different ships, participating in Civil War blockades and battles along the Virginia and North Carolina coasts. He joined the church in October 1867 and became an active member and later a leader and preacher at the Zion Wesley Church in Philadelphia. After service as an itinerant preacher, he was ordained as a deacon and assigned to churches in Baltimore; Washington, D.C.; and then Providence. In all assignments he helped the church grow by either saving troubled churches, founding new ones, or adding many new members. In 1888 he was elected presiding elder of the New England Conference, and, in addition to serving the Conference churches, contributed to many other A. M. E. Zion committees and conferences. Awarded a DD by Livingstone College in 1891, he wrote often for church publications and, at the time of his death, was working on an encyclopedia of the A. M. E. Zion Church.

Quiet and Revival

Save for the Railroad Street fire and the consequent departure of the Mason family, 1896 was a quiet year for the church. Activities were few until a new pastor, C. O. Waters, arrived in June. He had previously served in Attleboro, Massachusetts. There was the usual schedule of suppers and at east one musical/literary performance; in addition, a subscription drive produced $83 in December. In September Anderson Lewis and Jennie Suma were married in the church, the ceremony followed by a reception at the home of Mrs. Minerva Newport on Bridge Street. The year was significant for the A. M. E. Zion denomination, since it marked their first

This photograph was taken in the mid-1890s by Rev. Chauncey Hatfield. It is probably of a church group on the annual outing to Lake Buell. Source: Gary Levielle Collection, Great Barrington Historical Society.

one hundred years. Reverend Waters attended ceremonies marking the achievement in New York City on 1 October.

The year 1897 was, like the previous one, relatively tranquil. In May 1897 Reverend Waters was replaced by Rev. W. H. Parker. The church lost two valuable members when Mrs. Francis Newport died in April and Miss Lulu Jackson, an 1896 graduate of the high school, died in June. In July the church hosted a Spiritual Feast, with the United Methodist minister M. B. Snyder offering the sermon. Reverend Parker returned the favor in August when he preached at the Methodist Church. In September W. E. B. Du Bois visited, as did former pastor J. W. Hutchings in October.

The year ended with the Sunday school Christmas exercises, including songs by the class and recitations by Master C. Jackson, Master F. Suma, Miss N. Freeman, Miss E. Jackson, Master R. Sharpe, and Miss J. Smith. This list suggests a changing membership in the church, some children being from old families (Jackson, Suma, Freeman) and others from new ones (Sharpe and Smith).

The following year (1898) continued the same pattern of relatively few publicly announced events, and services were canceled for several weeks in February while Reverend Parker assisted with a revival in Derby, Connecticut. In June the New England Conference appointed James Young the pastor, and he and his wife immediately began to make changes in the church. The Sunday school was reorganized, R. Jones was elected superintendent, and, in July, a well-attended song service was offered. The names on the program included several ones that had not appeared before—Miss Edwards, Mrs. Moore, Miss Young, Miss Croslear, Mr. Austyn, Mrs. Lewis—suggesting a continuing change in church membership. In July another change took place when Presiding Elder S. C. Burchman of New Haven conducted his first Quarterly Conference, having replaced the deceased reverend Nathaniel Greene. On 5 August the church was again visited by Bishop J. W. Hood and his wife, the couple staying at the home of Mrs. Burget. On 18 August the *Courier* reported on the successful efforts of the new pastor:

> *Rev. Mr. Young and his wife in the short time they have been here, have accomplished a great deal of work. The church has been thoroughly cleaned and received a coat of paint on the exterior, which was much needed. A new kitchen has been added which is also a great improvement. A Christian Endeavor Society has been organized, also a new choir, and our colored people begin to attend to their own place of worship.*

In addition, dime suppers were offered more often, attendance increased, a musical performance was staged in November, and the pastor announced plans for a revival the following year. Several years of decay and neglect had been reversed in a few months.

1899—The Year of Revivals

The final year of the century opened with revival services during the second and third weeks of January led by Reverend Young, who was assisted by Rev. George Washington of Danbury, Connecticut. In May Rev. Isaac Watkins from Danbury replaced James Young as pastor and preached his first sermon. On 24 May Burghardt Gomer Du Bois, the fourteen-month-old son of W. E. B. and Nina Gomer Du Bois, died in Atlanta. The child's body was brought back to Great Barrington (where he was born) and buried in an unmarked grave in Mahaiwe Cemetery. A cross marking the grave was added later, and a historical marker for his and his mother's, Nina Gomer Du Bois's, graves erected in 1994.

On 22 June, plans for a large revival (camp meeting) at Abbey's Grove on the Van Deusenville Road to run from 30 July to 6 August were announced in the *Courier:*

There is to be preaching by able preachers from outside,
and excellent singing by jubilee singers and other devotional
exercises each day. The admission fee which will be charged, is
for the purpose of paying the incidental expenses and to help
the local church.

The revival went off as scheduled and benefited from pleasant weather and a large attendance. The preachers were, from Massachusetts, Rev. S. Johnson of Sheffield and Rev. Hilroy of Lee; E. L. Coffin; H. O. Lucas; and Dr. Brazil Watts, "the blind theologian" of Ansonia, Connecticut. Preaching was at ten thirty in the morning, three o'clock in the afternoon, and, in the evening, at six thirty at the grove and eight o'clock in the town hall, with a love feast ceremony at two o'clock in the afternoon. Jubilee singers provided the music. Participants were taken by carriage from the post office each hour, beginning at nine o'clock in the morning.

A major success, the meeting raised $175 for the church, which was applied to the mortgage and the pastor's salary. But there was also controversy:

There is some criticism of the lack of interest and co-operation
on the part of the church trustees, who naturally were expected

to lend every effort for the success of the camp meeting
enterprise, but who are reported by others as holding aloof from
it. The church membership in general[,[and the stewardesses
in particular, have done all in their power for the enterprise.
(Berkshire Courier *3 August 1899, 6)*

Camp meetings, like this one, were a popular form of worship in the United States in the nineteenth century. The first camp meeting of general significance took place in Cane Ridge, Kentucky, in 1801. Meetings were especially popular in the South, attended by whites and their black slaves. Efforts to keep the two groups segregated were rarely fully successful, and Black forms of worship including emotional preaching, singing, giving testimony, and free forms of worship became key elements of camp meetings. After the Civil War, Black churches organized their own meetings, with the A. M. E. Zion Church establishing a meeting at Tuckers Grove, North Carolina, in 1876. The Clinton meeting in 1899 was in this tradition.

The church ended the year by building on the success of the camp meeting. In September a fair and lawn party was held, in October a sparrow and gold ring supper, in November the quarterly meeting, and later in November a people's reception.

CHAPTER 4

Declines and Revivals
of the Early Twentieth Century

The Clinton Church survived two crises in the first two decades of the twentieth century. The first occurred in the early years of the new century as the number of members decreased and the church was damaged by the questionable financial activities of its pastor John I. A. D. LeChia. Over the next few years, under a series of more effective pastors, the church recovered and achieved some degree of stability, although a small and poor membership made raising enough money to support the church always a struggle. The second crisis was far more serious and began in 1913, when the Zion church actually ceased to exist and reincorporated as the Second Congregational Church of Great Barrington. The decision to switch denominational affiliation split the church membership, and in 1914 the A. M. E. Zion faction asserted itself with the help of the New England Conference and reestablished itself in its old home on Elm Court. Compared with these decades, the 1920s was a time of relative quiet for the church.

The twentieth century opened for the church just as the nineteenth century had ended, with difficulties between Rev. Isaac Watkins and the trustees. On 11 January the *Berkshire Courier* ran a long article headlined "Colored Preacher Locked Out." The article provides much insight into the contretemps between Reverend Watkins and three trustees, James Burghardt, Edward Wooster, and Anderson Lewis. Relations with trustee chairman Jason Cooley were more amicable. The headline referred to an incident the previous Sunday (7 January) when the trustees locked out the preacher, who was returning from conducting services in

Pittsfield, Massachusetts. The cause of the lockout was a dispute over entertainment hired by the trustees and advertised in the *Berkshire Eagle,* which the pastor deemed inappropriate for the church. The *Courier* (11 January, 5) described the planned entertainment by "Professor" Whiting and his two sons as "a program of novel and varied character, embracing a little of everything from Shakespearean 'dramaticals' to negro minstrelsy, and phrenology[,] or the examination of the diversified bumps of the human head." In Reverend Watkins's view, "such entertainments as that by 'Professor' Whiting and boys are not suited for the sanctuary at any time." Mainly because of confusion in placing the ads in the *Eagle* and the *Courier,* the entertainment was never staged.

The article also shed some light on the dispute of the previous fall concerning the camp meeting. Reverend Watkins was insulted that the trustees asked for a public accounting of the funds raised and especially their questioning his taking $75 of the proceeds for his salary. He pointed out that in the seven months he had been at the church, he had received only $41.25 in salary and was fully deserving of the additional $75. Reverend Watkins had no family and lived a frugal life in a boarding house on Bridge Street. He supplemented his church salary by preaching elsewhere and by selling shoe polish.

On 21 December 1900 the trustees sold the rear (westerly) portion of the Elm Court property to Charles E. Gorham (who had bought another parcel in 1886) and used the proceeds of $480 to pay off the mortgage held by the Great Barrington Savings Bank since 1887. Nonetheless, the dispute over both the pastor's salary and the form of entertainment appropriate for fund-raising for the church points to the continuing problem of raising enough money to support the church. A major cause of the financial problems was declining membership. In 1902 longtime member Mrs. L. M. Wooster noted in a letter to the *Courier* (30 October, 7) that the church had only seven members "and they [are] all women. Some are situated so they can not work much in the church and three of the seven are widows, all but one or two aged and invalids; three have small children to look after." This is probably an underestimate, for it ignores four or five men who served as trustees, but it was certainly true that the church had few members and most were elderly and poor.

The women of the Clinton church stayed apart from the difficulties and continued their schedule of dime suppers and special events, such as a pigeon pie supper, which involved a guest catching the live pigeon with a gold ring about its neck. In May the New England Conference reappointed Reverend Watkins, and in June he announced three camp meetings to be held in July and August at Abbey's grove. The meetings proved so successful that a fourth was added to the schedule, and in September Reverend Watkins announced that Sunday evening services would again be held regularly at the church, suggesting a new level of ministerial and financial stability.

Black Churches in Sheffield

One reason the Clinton membership was small in number was the existence of a series of Black churches in neighboring Sheffield. Sheffield had always had a relatively large Black community compared with other towns in the southern Berkshires. In 1855 Sheffield was home to some 142 Blacks. The community was large in part because Blacks had settled there after slavery was abolished in Massachusetts in 1783 to escape the slavery that continued in New York state and Connecticut for several more decades. The Sheffield community was split between those who lived in poverty, in the so-called New Guinea section of town around the intersection of Berkshire School Road and Bear's Den Road, and others who lived dispersed in other sections of town. And from this community the Clinton Church had always drawn some of its members. In fact, as mentioned in chapter one, it is possible that the local A. M. E. Zion Society was founded in the 1860s by a Black woman in Sheffield.

Information in the *Courier,* Sheffield town histories, and editions of the *Southern Berkshire Directory* suggests that Black preachers were in town in the 1860s and that a church serving the Black community of Sheffield was founded about 1885, was active until 1909, and then resumed as an active church from 1914 to 1916. The church was established when a chapel was built on Bear's Den Road in about 1885 with donations raised by Miss Georgia Andrus. The church was 15 feet by 20 and was described in the *Courier* in 1904: "No shanty is so humble but it has a picture of Abraham Lincoln and some scriptural quotations on the wall." The pastor lived in a cottage next door.

The denominational affiliation of the church evidently changed over the years, and it is not clear if the following names, taken from public records, accurately reflect the denomination affiliation of the church. It was at one time the Colored Southern Berkshire Holiness Society of New Guinea. In 1903 Charles Coffin is mentioned in the *Courier* as the minister from Sheffield. In 1905 Rev. A. M. deLuna is listed as the pastor of the New Guinea Church, and the following year he is listed as the pastor of the A. M. E. Bethel Church. In 1906 the church bought the existing property for $1, and the *Courier* reports on 19 April (p. 6) that revival services are to be held in "the new chapel" by Mrs. Grace Lee of Providence, Rhode Island. Lee had, in the previous month, held a revival at the Clinton Church. The 1907–1908 *Southern Berkshire Directory* lists the New Guinea A. M. E. Zion Church in Sheffield, with Rev. A. McKenzie as pastor. There was cooperation with the Clinton Church in Great Barrington:

> *On Tuesday, Wednesday and Thursday evenings of next week,*
> *the Ladies' Sewing Circle of the local A.M.E. Zion church will*
> *hold a fair at the church. Wednesday evening there will be a*
> *musical and literary entertainment in which Mary A. Carter,*
> *wife of the pastor of the church at New Guinea, Sheffield,*
> *"Philadelphia's favorite elecutionist" [sic] will appear, supported*
> *by local talent and the church choir. The doors open at 4p.m.*
> *Admission 10 cents.* (Berkshire Courier *20 August 1908, 3)*

The church closed in 1909 and reopened five years later, in 1914, again as a Zion church with Rev. B. W. Smith as pastor. Regular announcements in the *Courier* suggest that the church had an active membership and a Sunday school. In 1915 Rev. S. V. Holland replaced Reverend Smith, who became pastor of the Clinton Church. The Sheffield church closed in 1916, and the building later burned to the ground. Later editions of the *South Berkshire Directory* list the church but no minister or officers. Among those active in the church were Edward Augustus Croslear, a deacon and a Civil War veteran and leading Black citizen of the town; Edward Moore; and Frederick ("Fred") L. Freeman.

The LeChia Pastorate

In May 1901 the New England Conference reassigned Reverend Watkins and placed Rev. John I. A. D. LeChia at the church. Reverend LeChia was a man of considerable intellect and energy but also one given to grand but questionable schemes. LeChia set about to right the financial condition of the church and to expand the religious program. Almost every week an announcement in the *Courier* listed church activities for the coming Sunday, including a long list of sermons, to be given Sunday mornings and evenings:

Judas, an Enigma
A Good Soldier
Self-Examination
A Troubled Heart
How to Know the Goodness of God
A Noble Revolution
A Fatherless and Motherless Priest
A Spirit of Liberality
A Determined Man with the Right Idea
What Is Our Duty
A Prepared Home
When to Pray
The Perfect Felicity of the Resurrected Saints, a Result of Conformity
  and Divine Likeness
Claims of the Gospel Message
What Am I
The Negro's Past, Present and Future

The Sunday school was revived and began meeting every Sunday at two o'clock in the afternoon. In June the school staged a full program to celebrate Children's Day (*Berkshire Courier* 20 June, 3):

Sunday will be children's day at A.M.E. Zion church. The
exercises will begin at 11 o'clock with an organ voluntary by
Mrs. Emma Jackson, followed by exercises as follows: Recital
of Ten Commandments and Apostles' Creed, invocation, solo,

Hattie Peterson; reading, Priscilla Johnson; solo, Lillian Lewis;
recitation, Beatrice Sewell; selection, choir; recitation, Irene
Chinn; solo, Minnie Hoffman; infant Baptism; Lord's prayer,
congregation; solo, Emma Jackson; collection and address by
Rev. John LeChia; reading, Jennie Moore; solo, Elijah Austin;
recitation, Alice White; selection, choir; recitation, solo, Mary P.
LeChia; doxology, benediction. The subject of the sermon will be
"How to Know the goodness of God."

The church suppers continued, and a strawberry and ice cream festival
was held in June, and a social in July. All of this activity led Reverend Le-
Chia to claim on 27 June (*Berkshire Courier,* p. 3): "In his effort to secure
funds for the proposed Clinton A.M.E. Zion church parsonage, pastor Le-
Chia reports that he is meeting with excellent results." The plan to build
a parsonage is somewhat surprising given that the church still carried a
debt and could not afford to pay its pastor a full salary. Later accounting
was to show that the excellent results claimed by LeChia were actually
less than $80.

In August LeChia, who had trouble finding affordable housing for
himself, his wife, and daughter, rented rooms at the top of Railroad Street
and announced a plan to open an employment agency that would recruit
"colored" help from the South. The agency never got off the ground,
and LeChia evidently supported himself by other means, including sell-
ing book subscriptions and arranging concerts, an enterprise that often
took him away from Great Barrington and caused many Sunday morning
services to be canceled.

Looking back from our current perspective one hundred-some
years later, we see the first sign of trouble with LeChia's activities in the
5 September issue of the *Courier.* In a lengthy statement by Reverend
LeChia, there is the hint that questions were being raised about his activities and his fund-raising for the church.

Statement by Rev. LeChia. An Acounting for all Money Received
From the Recent Concerts.

Rev. LeChia, pastor of the A.M.E. Zion church of this place,
promised to give the people of Great Barrington a rare treat.

*This he has done under many difficulties and great expense
because he had promised, advertised and secured the hall for
this concert company. In order to get the company to Great
Barrington, he was compelled to secure other dates for them
which caused the pastor hard work, worry and expense. This
had to be liquidated by the proceeds of the concert given here.
The total receipts for the concerts from August 23 to August
30 were $395.55 of which $320.55 is the share of Rev. D. J.
Jenkins, manager of the Orphanage, leaving $70.00 which
Rev. LeChia paid out for halls, advertising, board, lodging, fare,
telephone and telegrams. This report is submitted that the
public may know that the A.M.E. Zion church of this place, or
its pastor, has not received one cent from this venture. But he
is satisfied that he has sustained his character and reputation
in the community where he is so arduously working for God and
His church.*

Another sign of trouble came three weeks later, when the *Courier* (26
September, 3) ran the following item making a claim that seems to be
highly unlikely: "Rev. J. I. A. D. LeChia of the A. M. E. Zion church is an
intimate acquaintance of President Roosevelt. When Mr. LeChia was pastor of the Zion church in Oyster Bay, the new president once spoke in his
church. On the return of Col. Roosevelt from Santiago, Mr. LeChia was
one of the first to call on the distinguished hero. Mr. LeChia has in his
possession several letters from President Roosevelt."

In October Reverend LeChia announced that he had collected $668
in the last quarter for the church. Again, later events tell us that this
was an exaggeration. Nonetheless, LeChia seems to have made a good
impression on the members of the church, and in May 1902 they wrote
the New England Conference asking that LeChia be reappointed pastor
for another year. The letter was published in the *Courier* on 8 May accompanied by an annual report for May 1901 to May 1902 prepared by
LeChia. The report shows a small membership, a very busy pastor, and
suggests that the financial situation was improving.

Members 8
Marriages 0
Deaths 2
Adults baptized 0
Children baptized... 4
Sermons preached 111
Pastoral visits... 72

Total Raised and Expended................. $854.40
Raised for relief fund 1.52
Raised for Children's Day.......................... 3.39
Raised for Easter...................................... 3.10
Raised for presiding elder....................... 18.85
Raised for general fund 7.40
Raised for Sunday school convention......... 4.50
Raised for Sunday school........................... 7.98
Raised for current expenses 76.46
Raised for conference claims.................. 10.00
Raised for pastor's salary...................... 226.86

Mortgage 0.00
Floating debt.. 297.35

In October LeChia suddenly left the church and town, claiming that he was forced to do so because the church was not paying him his salary. He relocated to Hoboken, New Jersey, with his travel expenses evidently paid from Great Barrington's poor fund. The editor of the *Courier* (30 October, 1) saw LeChia as the culprit rather than the victim:

Deadbeats

Those acquaintances of Rev. John A. I. D. LeChia, who lately vacated the pulpit of the Clinton A. M. E. Zion church, who think he was more sinned against than sinning in, that his church did not furnish him money to exist on, will be interested in the letter from Mrs. Wooster, a most estimable colored lady, which appears on another page. LeChia was simply a loafer, blowhard and beat. It suited him better to beat his landlord out of house rent and his grocer out of provisions than it would to have had rent and garden free from Mrs. Wooster. In that respect he was just like other deadbeats, white as well as colored. By the way, there are plenty white ones in town.

Mrs. Wooster's letter took a full column on page seven and is instructive for both what it tells us about LeChia's tenure and for what it tells us about Black life in Great Barrington in the early twentieth century. The Woosters lived at this time in the Burghardt house on South Egremont Road. One of the visitors Mrs. Wooster refers to in her letter was W. E. B. Du Bois, who visited her in late September or early October 1901, staying in the house that had previously been his grandparents and would become his in 1928.

Editor Courier: I would like to say a few words in reference to Pastor LeChia, who left so suddenly a couple of weeks ago, and also about the church here. It certainly is, as you say, a very weak church, there being but seven members and they all women. Some are situated so they cannot work much in the church and three of the seven are widows, all but one or two aged and invalids: three have small children to look after.[Among the female members were Lula Williams, the Gunn and Allen sisters, and Irene Chinn.] The trustees have their duties to perform and on account of the weakness of the church and so much lameness and sickness among the people I proposed to the pastor's family, which heard I was looking for a tenement where their child could play on the ground, that they spend the summer with me as I was alone and very anxious to have someone with me. I told them I would give them their rent from the time he came from conference and also a garden. I had a horse fertilizer, etc., which they could use. I said I would give them their rent until in October after the produce was gathered, and possibly for the winter, but said my son might be home with his wife and that then I might have to make different arrangements. I told them I would give them a large sleeping room—large enough for three beds—and she could use the kitchen, parlor and sitting room in connection with me, but she seemed to think he must have my spare room for a study. As she wanted to have a single bed in it I concluded it was for napping. I told her I couldn't spare it as I sometimes had company. I told him he would have to work sharp in his garden, as I attended mine myself and raised what I could to sell, but my daughter's little dog barked snappishly at his little girl and that exasperated him very much. I told him that I would clean up the dog but that they must keep their child away from him as he wasn't used to being poked by children. I told him to send me word if he wanted the house, but he sent word that he wouldn't want it as he had another place in view where he could be near his church, which did not seem to me very important as he held but very few meetings there except on Sunday nights.

I proposed a grove meeting but he opposed it on account of the iniquity there might be going on outside. I told him he must expect Satan to do his work, whatever work the church was in. A union tent meeting he wouldn't assist in on the Sabbath afternoon as he didn't want, he said, to leave the Pickanniny band. I hope he will do more good in Hoboken than he has done here. He has had all the money there has been raised excepting for a little oil. He refused to attend to the church so Lewis Ferris was hired for that. I don't know whether he has received any money or not yet. We supposed LeChia had funds in hand, as he told us how much repairing he was going to do at the church as he had great influence with some rich white gentleman and when the time came to develop the secret to the trustees we would all know what he had done for the benefit of the church.

Mrs. L. M. Wooster

Mrs. Wooster's motivation in writing this letter is not known, but it seems to be an attempt to distance the church from LeChia and to make a public statement that the members held LeChia in the same low regard as did the town in general.

Subsequent reports in the *Courier* disclosed that LeChia had debt problems at his previous posting in Danbury, Connecticut, had obtained books for sale fraudulently while in Great Barrington, and several years later spent time in the "Tombs" (correctional facility) in New York City.

LeChia was quickly replaced by Reverend Watkins, his predecessor, and on 11 December the *Courier* ran an anonymous letter, lauding the high quality of the church suppers:

HAD LOTS OF GOOD EATING

High Praise for the Ladies of the A. M. E. Zion
Church From One of Their Supper Patrons

The following communication got "lost in the shuffle"—the
church ladies must excuse the expression; we mean lost in the
shuffle incident to moving; as a consequence its publication
was belated. However, a compliment so well bestowed will be
appreciated, we've no doubt, even at this late day:

Editor Berkshire Courier: Having always been taught to pass on
a good thing when it costs nothing to do so, I beg to be allowed
to put the principle into operation.

The other night, I was invited to a "ten-cent" supper at the
A. M. E. Zion church. I went. I expected beans, pickles and coffee.
I ate chicken-pie, cabbage salad, rolls and coffee, and ice cream
and cake.

The pie was good; it appeared to be chicken-pie as distinguished
from hen-pie. The rolls and butter were as good as those served
in the best hotels and the ice cream and cake were fully up to
the standard. The salad was not merely wilted cabbage with
vinegar on it, but a well seasoned article.

The room where this "ten-cent" supper was served was small
but well ventilated and lighted, and the service was good.

When I leaned back in my chair and contemplated my empty ice-cream plate. I was ashamed to look the cashier in the face. I have eaten the suppers served by every church society in town and never before got so much for my money by one hundred percent.

If the A. M. E. Zion society should ever advertise a 25-cent supper it would pay the consolidated road to run special transportation for I am sure there would be spread for the public a better supper than could be procured anywhere in the country for a dollar bill.

Observer.

The apparent intent of the letter was to assist the struggling church by encouraging whites in town to attend the church suppers.

Stabilization under Reverend Watkins and his Successors

Despite his claims, Rev. LeChia left the church in worse condition than it had been when he took over eighteen months earlier. The church was broke, the membership small and poor, the building run down, and water collected in the basement when it rained. The water problem was caused by the location of the church at the bottom of a hill. The area across Elm Court (now the Berkshire Bank parking lot) was at one time a pond.

Reverend Watkins and his successors (Rev. W. B. Caines, 1903–1904; Rev. J. A. Curtis, 1904–1905; Rev. David R. Overton, 1905–1908; Rev. S. E. Robinson, 1909–1912; and Samuel H. Johnson, 1912–1913) all followed the same general strategy in trying to increase income and maintain the church building. The strategy involved regular suppers, fund-raising entertainment provided by outside talent, greater involvement with the local community and churches, and special events. Among the special events were these:

Banjo performance by Reverend Coffin of Sheffield in February 1903
Performance by the Stockbridge Symphony in April 1903
Lecture by Rev. J. F. Waters of Brooklyn in August 1903

Concert by Mrs. Flossie Freeman of New Bedford, MA, in August 1905

Revival service by Mrs. Grace Lee of Providence in March 1906

Lecture by Rev. D. J. F. Moreland, manager of the Zion Publications House in July 1907

Music and Readings by Mary Carter of Philadelphia in August 1908 and March 1909

Lecture by Bishop Alexander Walters of New York in July 1909

Concert by Hampton Institute students in August 1910

Choir concert with violinist and soloists in August 1912

The pastors also forged closer relations with other churches. In August 1904 the presiding bishop J. W. Hood visited and prominent members of the community, including Congregational minister L. D. Bliss, and Mr. J. F. Whiting, attended the reception fore the Bishop and entertainment; in September the D. G. Anderson post of the GAR (Grand Army of the Republic) attended a service marking the anniversary of emancipation. Reverend and Mrs. E. H. Todd of North Egremont provided stereopticon entertainment in October 1906 and January 1907. And in February 1912 Mrs. R. J. Logan gave an organ (piano) to the church.

The strategy, the hard work of the pastors, and support of the congregation paid off, and the church solved some its problems and achieved some stability. By the middle of 1905 Reverend Curtis had raised enough money to connect the cellar to the sewer line, alleviating the flooding problem. On 6 June 1907 the trustees obtained a mortgage of $600 from John Viola. Viola was a mason and contractor who had come from Italy to the United States in 1870, and to Great Barrington in 1871. The deed was signed by trustees Cooley, Lewis, and Wooster and was later sold to the Great Barrington Savings Bank and paid off in 1921. By November the church had raised nearly $100 to pay off its debt, a sizable sum considering the size of the church membership, its limited resources, and the need to use much of what was raised to support the church and pay the pastor.

During these early years of the twentieth century, the church also increased its membership to about twenty people. The 1907–1908 *Southern Berkshire Directory* lists seven officers and trustees:

Trustees: ....Jason Cooley,
                         Edward Wooster Jr.
                         Anderson Lewis
Clerk:.....................George Hyatt
Sunday school
  superintendent:...Mrs. Helen Hyatt
Secretary:..............Mrs. Henrietta Freeman
Treasurer: ....Bertha Brown

The 1910–1911 *Southern Berkshire Directory* shows the trustees and officers having increased to eight positions:

Trustees: ....Jason Cooley,
                         Edward Wooster Jr.,
                         Anderson Lewis,
                         James Calhoun,
                         Isaac Lewis
Clerk:.....................Gerald Sewell
Sunday School
  Superintendent:...George Hyatt
Sunday School
  Assistant: ....Mrs. Milton (Emma) Jackson

Other members during these years were Edward Ferris, George H. Jackson, Daniel Brown Jr., Mabel Gunn, Lena Wooster, Jennie Moore, Bertha Berry, and Lula Williams. Church services were at eleven in the morning and eight in the evening on Sunday, with Sunday school at four in the afternoon. Reverend Overton lived in a house at the rear of 9 Rosseter Street; number 9 in 2006 was the home of the Macedonia Baptist Church, and the small yellow building behind it may have been the building that housed Rev. Overton. The most prominent of these members were probably Jason Cooley and George Jackson. Jackson owned a restaurant at 327 Main Street, which he advertised in the directory.

Perhaps the strongest sign of stability was the announcement in the 6 August 1909 *Courier* (p. 3) in the "Church Announcements" column:

An ad for George Jackson's Jackson Restaurant placed in the 1908 *Southern Berkshire Directory.*

"Sunday services at the A.M.E. Zion church by Rev. S. E. Robinson. Preaching at 10.45, Sunday school at 12.30 pm. Prayer and conference meeting at 7.30 conducted by Mr. Hyatt." This is the first time in many years that the church's service was listed in this column along with those of the other Great Barrington churches. And the regular activity in the church meant that it again was the hub of religious and social activities in the Great Barrington Black community. It is important to remember that while the Elm Court–Rosseter neighborhood was home to some Blacks, the membership lived all over town: Edward Ferris on Stockbridge Road, George Jackson on Castle Lane, Daniel Brown on Railroad Row, Mabel Gunn and Jennie Moore on Rosseter Street, the Woosters on South Egremont Road, the Cooleys on East Street, the Isaac Lewises on Pine Street, and Anderson and Ella Lewis and George and Helen Hyatt on Main Street. It was not until the 1930s that the area around the church became the town's "Black" neighborhood, although even then it remained integrated.

The increase in members led to an increase in the social and service clubs associated with the church, which, during the first decade of the century, included the Sewing Society, the Young Ladies' Guild, the Willing Workers, the Organ Guild, Young People's Lyceum, Ladies' Aid Society, the Oak Leaf Club, and the Silver Leaf Musical Club. All of the these organizations ran fund-raising events for the church, although the core fund-raisers were always the "ladies" of the church and their regular chicken, turkey, and oyster suppers; ice cream and strawberry socials; and teas.

From Zion to Congregationalism and then back to Zion

Despite all this effort and the greater acceptance in the Great Barrington community, the financial situation remained difficult. A notice in the 1 September 1910 *Courier* mentioned that a rally was planned to raise money to pay off some of the $500 mortgage. Although, as mentioned above, in 1902 LeChia reported that there was no debt, this $500 was evidently the balance of the 1907 Viola mortgage. Church fund-raising activities were bringing in about $600 per year, and this covered only a portion of the pastor's salary and some of the operating expenses. Most of the $600 came from nonmembers who attended the suppers and socials and the entertainment arranged by the church. By now the church was in need of repair and needed a new coat of paint on the exterior.

In either 1912 or 1913 Rev. John E. Hill replaced Reverend Johnson. While the traditional sorts of money-raising events and services continued in early 1913, by the spring or perhaps even earlier, Reverend Hill became convinced that the Clinton Church had little future as part of the A. M. E. Zion Church. He proposed to the membership, almost surely with the encouragement of leading white citizens, that the church end its ties to the A. M. E. Zion church and affiliate instead with Congregationalism. In Great Barrington at the time, many leading citizens were members of the Congregational Church, although others belonged to the Episcopal and Roman Catholic churches. The debate over Reverend Hill's radical proposal split the membership, which Hill claimed to be twenty-eight people. Some of those who refused to agree were expelled. By June Hill had succeeded and the Zion church transferred its property to the Second Congregational Church (Registry of Deeds, vol. 211, 356):

Know all Men by the Presents,

That We, the Trustees of the African Methodist Episcopal Zion Church of Great Barrington, Berkshire County, Massachusetts, a religious association existing and owning property in said

Great Barrington under the laws of the Commonwealth of
Massachusetts in consideration of one Dollar ($1.00) paid
by the Second Congregational Church of Great Barrington,
Massachusetts . . . do hereby give, grant, sell and convey unto
the said Second Congregational Church of Great Barrington . . .
the church premises of said society with the church building . . .
[a]lso hereby conveying to the Second Congregational Church of
Great Barrington, Massachusetts, all books, furniture, fixtures,
cash-on-hand, credits, and accounts due or to become due and
payable to said society, and all other personal property, rights
and assets of every name and nature. This conveyance is made
under authority of a vote of said society passed at a meeting
legally called and held on June twenty-fifth, 1913.

[. . .]

In Witness Whereof, the said Trustees of the African Methodist
Episcopal Zion Church of Great Barrington, Massachusetts
Have hereunto set their hands and seals this   day of June
In the year of our Lord one thousand nine hundred and thirteen.

Signed, Sealed and delivered in presence of

	Edward W. Wooster & Seal
	Jennie E. Moore & Seal
John E. Hill	*Sarah E. Lewis & Seal*
	Helen M. Hyatt & Seal
	George W. Hyatt & Seal

The event was important in town and drew a page-one article in the
Courier on 19 June summarizing the new arrangement:

ZION CHURCH NO MORE

Has Been Adopted into the Great
Congregational Family and Will
Hereafter be Known as the Second

Congregational Church of Great
Barrington. — Formal Service of
Recognition Held Friday. — To
Be Incorporated.

The Great Barrington A.M.E. Zion church is such no longer. It
has thrown off the yoke of Zion and gone over body and soul to
Congregationalism, and henceforth will be known as the Second
Congregational church of Great Barrington.

The council was held on June 5, and the representative
Congregational churches of the county were part of that council.
After considerable discussion of the topic it was voted to accept
the Zion church in Congregational fellowship under the change
of name and last Friday evening, at the Zion church, a service of
recognition was held. The Rev. Leon D. Bliss of Lenox, moderator
of the council, also presided at this service of recognition. The
service was preached by the Rev. Oliver D. Sewall, pastor of the
First Congregational church of Great Barrington. The address
to the pastor, Rev. J. E. Hill, was delivered by the Rev. Mr. Baker
of Pittsfield. The address of welcome was delivered by the
Rev. Leon D. Bliss. Prayer was made by the Rev. Silas Cook of
Pittsfield, county missionary.

The service was quite largely attended and the church will on
June 25, be duly incorporated. An interesting program was
carried out at the service of recognition in the way of music,
special selections were given by the choir, and it was a service
that will long be memorable to the colored people of the town,
thus received into Congregationalism, for the change was
brought about only after a long and vigorous fight of the local
organization against the Zion religious body, which strenuously
objected to the Great Barrington church seceding.

The colored, people, generally, are pleased over the change, for
the majority of them were Congregationalists from the outset,
and in having their church recognized formally and accepted

by the Congregational council, they believe will be the means
of strengthening them materially, as the church has long been
weak in membership and poor in finances.

This article requires some consideration here, since it tells us something
about the conditions that led to the reaffiliation of the church and the
attitudes of white citizens toward the Zion church. The phrases "It has
thrown off the yoke of Zion" and "for the majority of them were Congregationalists from the outset" suggest that the Clinton Church had never
enjoyed full acceptance in the town. This conclusion is supported by
infrequent placement over the years of church announcements in the
"Church Happenings" column of the *Courier.*

Further, the statement about the majority being Congregationalists is
not supported by any known evidence. In the 1870s when the Zion Society was established in Great Barrington, W. E. B. Du Bois and his mother,
Mary Burghardt Du Bois, were the only Black members of the Congregational Church. Prior to the founding of the Zion Society few Blacks
belonged to churches—and those who did attended the Congregational
churches or the Episcopal church in town or the Congregational Church
in neighboring South Egremont. In addition, many of the early members
were recent arrivals from the South and would not have had much expo-
sure to Congregationalism.

The above article plus the following one, which appeared on page
2 of the *Courier* on 14 August, suggest that white people in town were
feeling burdened by the Clinton Church. It had not been self-supporting
for at least a decade and had a small membership, and the building had
become run-down. Affiliation with Congregationalism was probably
viewed by some as a way of gaining the church wider acceptance in the
community, of drawing more members, of attracting large contributions
from the community, and perhaps as a symbolic act that reflected a wish
by the membership for a new beginning.

A Worthy Project

Second Congregational Church is Seeking to Pay Off its Church
Debt and Build a Parsonage — Has Organized Company of
Jubilee Singers to Aid.

Since the Rev. J. E. Hill took the pastorate of the society, the Second Congregational church, the colored church of Great Barrington, has taken upon itself a new lease of life. Mr. Hill found the organization much run down and started to build it up. He began the building by impressing on the minds of his people the necessity of doing their best toward becoming self-sustaining so far as they could do so. The fire of his enthusiasm enkindled others, with the result that interest in the organization has deepened and its activities have greatly increased.

The church has a present membership of twenty-eight. It raises itself upward of $600 per year from pledges among its members and in various ways, but all of this sum goes toward paying the annual upkeep of the church and society, including pastor's salary, running expenses, etc., as well as its contributions toward the work of missions. It is, however, a hard, uphill struggle.

The church has a debt of $500 which it wants to liquidate. It also feels the need of a parsonage, and the Rev. Mr. Hill and his official board of church workers are desirous of raising $4,000 with which to clear off this debt, and also build a parsonage. For this purpose the society has organized a troup [sic] of jubilee singers and are giving concerts and entertainments wherever they can help raise funds for the church debt and parsonage fund. The entertainments are of good class and most entertaining. They comprise jubilee and plantation songs, sung with the peculiar fitness characteristic of the Negro race, and they hope to aid materially the finances of the church.

Mr. Hill has been strenuously impressing upon his people the need of helping themselves first before asking aid of the public. It was through him that the society swung over from Zionism to Congregationalism, and the change was brought about only after much difficulty in getting things properly adjusted to their new environment. Mr. Hill and his people believe that with patient work along the lines laid down, that there is a good future ahead of the church, and he is seeking to bring about the much

*desired results. Any aid that may be given the organization in
way of contributions will be appreciated or any society desiring
to aid the project through entertainment of jubilee songs will
find on consulting Mr. Hill that arrangements can be made for
such. The church will appreciate any co-operation that will aid
it in carrying out its projects.*

Reverend Hill got to work making changes, and by October the church
had been painted and plans were under way for a new chimney. But not
all members were happy with the new arrangement, and neither was the
New England Conference. In December the Conference sent Rev. Sidney
L. Smith to Great Barrington to represent the Zion Church's interests in
Great Barrington and Sheffield (the Sheffield church had closed in 1909).
Reverend Smith was young but was well-educated (Livingstone College
and Boston University School of Theology); had been successful in paying
off the mortgage at the church in Plainsville, Connecticut; and his uncle
was a bishop in the Zion Church. The Church was taking the loss of the
Great Barrington church quite seriously and had carefully picked the
man to make it right. Reverend Smith must have begun right to work
with the unhappy members, expelling them; on 18 December the *Courier* (p. 3) noted that "the trouble at the Second Congregational church,
formerly A. M. E. Zion church, will it is feared, disrupt the church if not
speedily settled." The trouble centered on the ongoing dispute between
Reverend Hill, with his supporters, and the Zion faction that wanted to
remain in the Zion fold and that suspected Hill's main motivation was the
new parsonage; the faction believed that he had less interest in the well-
being of the church than he claimed. The conflict worsened when some
in the Zion faction removed the organ from the church, claiming that it
was personal, not church property.

To help settle the dispute and to further Hill's wishes for a parsonage, Warren H. Davis, a Black lumber dealer and land speculator, offered to take the former Zion property and building, in return providing
the new church with land and a new church and parsonage near the
Dewey School. Davis, however, refused to assume the $600 mortgage
that had been transferred from the Clinton Zion to the Second Congregational Church. On 23 December the church members voted to convey
the church property to Davis, and on the following day a warranty deed

An advertisement for Warren Davis's lumber business placed in the 1914 *Southern Berkshire Directory*.

legalized the transfer. The deed stipulated that Davis would not use the premises for "church purposes" but made no mention of his promise to build a new church and parsonage near the Dewey School (Registry of Deeds, vol. 215, 17). The deed was signed for the church by Hill and the trustees (Della Wright, Ella E. Lewis, Helen Anderson, and John Hill [the pastor's father]).

Warren Davis (1884–1960) was a land speculator and lumber dealer and one of the first Black entrepreneurs in the region. Born in North Carolina, he moved to Great Barrington as a young man. He attended school in town and worked for the inventor William Stanley. After attending the Massachusetts Agricultural College in Amherst (now the University of Massachusetts at Amherst), he opened a lumber business. For much of his adult life, he lived at 11 Rosseter Street in Great Barrington and, from about 1907 until the late 1950s, operated out of an office in his home and also on occasion from one on Main Street. At times he owned sizable tracts of forest in western Massachusetts, northern Connecticut, and eastern New York state. He was a major supplier of lumber to local yards and to the railroad, and he owned much of the land that became Beartown State Forest. Davis also owned a nightclub, the Harlem Inn in Copake, New York, where entertainment was provided by live bands and dancing on weekends. Sometimes a wealthy man, he lived a modest life on Rosseter Street. He never married but lived for many years with

Mabel Gunn (1885–1959), who was also his bookkeeper. Mabel Gunn was a significant local figure in her own right, active in the Red Cross and the NAACP. An award in her name was established by the Pittsfield office of the NAACP in 1960. Warren Davis died at the Gunn homestead in Stockbridge on 30 November 1960 after a brief illness.

The result of the deal was that the church no longer had a home or property and still owed $600 on the mortgage. Nonetheless, Rev. Hill "expressed the opinion that the society has the long end of the bargain" (*Berkshire Courier* 1 January 1914, 1). Davis, in turn, moved to sell the former Zion property to a third party.

Members of the Zion faction responded quickly, and on 21 January 1914 their attorney H. Newton Joyner brought action before the Superior Court in *John E. Hill et al. v. Edward M. Wooster et al.* In addition to Wooster action members comprised Joseph Jaynes, Sarah Ferris, Laura Suma, Marie Sewall, Mary Jackson, Katie West, Lena Wooster, Susan Jaynes, Mary Rogers, Josephine Van Buren, Katherine Lewis, and Alice Churchill. Named as defendants were John E. Hill, Della Wright, Ella E. Lewis, Helen Anderson, John P. Hill, Warren H. Davis, and George L. Taylor.

The matter was resolved in the Zion faction's favor at a meeting of the membership held at the First Congregational Church on 12 February 1914.

*The members of the Second Congregational Church (colored)
who were expelled some time ago in the church disaffection,
which has for some time been in progress, were reinstated at the
meeting held at the chapel of the First Congregational church last
Thursday night. These officers were then elected: Clerk, George
Hyatt; treasurer, Edward M. Wooster; trustees, Mrs. Jennie Moore,
George Hyatt, Joseph Jaynes, Mrs. George Hyatt and Mrs. Lena
Wooster. The Rev. Mr. Hill was deposed from the pastorate by the
election of the Rev. Sidney Smith as the pastor of the church until
a permanent pastor is decided upon. Now the controlling faction
of the church has the right to worship in the church and will do so.
There has been considerable splitting up of the society under Mr.
Hill's pastorate, and when he, with others of his adherents, sold
the church property to Warren H. Davis, who in turn mortgaged it
to another party, and the case got into the courts, matters became
further complicated and it will take some time before the legal*

> *muddle is made straight. Meanwhile the Zion preacher seems to*
> *have control of the present church machinery and may eventually*
> *become the permanent pastor of the society.*

On 26 April a revival service was held in the church on Elm Court, followed on 17 May by a rededication service with Presiding Elder C. S. Whited preaching the sermon. The Zion Society also prevailed in court, and on 2 May, on Justice of the Peace George L. Taylor's order, the Second Congregational Church sold the property to the A. M. E. Zion Church of America for $1, thereby closing this unfortunate episode in the church's history. The national church held the property until 1945, when it was sold for $1 to the local church.

The A. M. E. Zion Church was also able to reopen the church in Sheffield, and on 2 July the Rev. B. W. Smith held services there for the first time in five years, with services being announced for every Sunday in the following months. In Great Barrington the church again set about raising funds, but an announcement in the *Courier* on 5 November (p. 3) suggests that the church had not yet built a chimney and could not remain open in the winter months: "Rev. T. H. Jones of the Methodist Church extends an invitation to the members of the congregation of the A. M. E. Zion church, which has been closed until next May, to attend services at the Methodist church."

Burning the Mortgage

The church reopened in May 1915 with Rev. B. W. Smith as pastor. Smith had formerly reestablished the church in Sheffield and was replaced there by Rev. S. V. Holland. Both Reverend Smith and his wife had attended seminaries, and both preached in the Clinton Church. Newspaper accounts suggest that Mrs. Smith was an especially able preacher, with the *Courier* noting on 27 May (p. 3) that "Mrs. Smith is considered both eloquent and interesting." Having a ministerial couple available added to the spiritual life of the church, and Rev. Smith was also eager to retire the mortgage. The play *Can You Make Me Happy Forever?* was staged on Memorial Day, the renowned African American tenor Sydney Woodward performed at town hall in September, and the Christian Endeavor Society staged short versions of the popular drama *Way Down East* twice in September. *Way*

Down East would have been an especially meaningful play for a Berkshire audience. It extolled the virtues of small-town New England life and criticized the corruption and classism of city life. In 1920 it was released as a popular silent film by the noted director D. W. Griffiths.

Evidently the church closed for several months again in the winter of 1915–1916. Services resumed in April 1916. The Holiness movement, which had started to spread around the world from the Azusa Street Revival in Los Angeles ten years earlier, had a major impact on the A. M. E. Zion Church. That impact was seen during the year 1916 in the Clinton Church with an indoor Georgia-style camp meeting in August, an Alabama-style big meeting in September, preaching by the evangelist Harry Dearing in September and December, and preaching by John Decker of the Salvation Army in November. In addition, Mrs. Seline Hector and Mrs. Hayward Suma were baptized in the Housatonic River at the foot of Dresser Avenue in August, and Mr. and Mrs. Nelson Piper in September.

The campaign to reduce the debt, which now stood at only $165, resumed as well. Reverend C. M. Starkweather of the Methodist Church assisted with a stereopticon performance of the *Passion Play* in May, and in September the church hosted two debates, entitled "Who has Done More for the Negro Race, Abraham Lincoln or Booker T. Washington?" Also in September, Miss Cora Fowler recited from the poems of Paul Lawrence Dunbar. Fowler was likely the first Black schoolteacher in the county when, in 1903, she was hired to teach in the planned Black-only school in Sheffield. Her career was short, however, since Black parents boycotted the segregated school and it soon burned down one night.

Dunbar, whose poetry Fowler read, was one the first African American poets whose work was popular with African Americans and whites. He was born in Dayton, Ohio, in 1872 and died there at the age of thirty-three from tuberculosis in 1906. The child of former slaves from Kentucky, and unable to attend college because the family was too poor, he began writing poetry as a teenager and also wrote novels and music. He wrote in both Black southern English dialect and standard English, with the plantation experiences of his mother informing much of his work. Among his collections are *Oak and Ivy, Majors and Minors, Folks from Dixie, Lyrics of Love and Laughter,* and *Howdy, Honey, Howdy.* His style influenced later Harlem Renaissance writers such as Countee Cullen (who was wed briefly to Du Bois's daughter) and Langston Hughes.

During these years there were also some changes in the governing body of the church. Edward Wooster, Nelson Piper, Fred Freeman, J. Thompson, and George Mallory were now the trustees, with Mrs. B. W. Smith serving as treasurer and secretary and Freeman as Sunday school superintendent. In 1917 there was a change in pastors when Reverend and Mrs. Smith left suddenly for Newark, New Jersey, in late February and were replaced in the summer by Rev. Byron Scott. The year was marked as well by a sizable increase in the Black population in the county, with the *Courier* (12 July, 1) reporting the arrival of several hundred Blacks from the South, the men working on farms and on railroad construction and the women as domestics and in hotels and restaurants.

The next few years were slow ones for the church. Reverend Scott remained pastor until 1920, when Rev. William H. Martin replaced him, and then Scott returned to the pastorate in 1921. One interesting item of news was the arrest of the former pastor, Rev. John Hill, for loafing in August 1918. Hill, who had been removed as pastor after leading the unsuccessful affiliation with Congregationalism, evidently remained in town and had been working as a laborer and living at 44 Pearl Street. In 1920 the trustees were Mrs. Jennie Moore and Fred Freeman.

Reverend Martin renewed the effort to pay off the mortgage with a series of services in September 1920, which drew many people from town. The effort continued in June 1921 with a series of "entertainments," including a recital by Reverend Martin and church members, a singing program, a performance of "The Call to Service," readings, and a chicken pie supper. The effort continued under Rev. Scott in August with a concert and other entertainment and then two special song services in September. Finally, on 2 October 1921, "at the services at the A. M. E. Zion church Sunday evening the church mortgage [held by the Great Barrington Savings Bank] was burned as a result of the solicitation of funds for the purpose by the pastor, Rev. Byron Scott."

The 1920s

By 1920 the Great Barrington population had increased to 6,315 and then, by 1925, to 6,405 according to the state census. The Black share of the population remained small and disproportionately elderly, although large enough to contemplate forming a Black Knights of Pythias Lodge in 1922; to field a baseball team, the Colored Giants, in 1925; and to hold a ball in the town hall in September 1928. For half of the decade Byron Scott was the pastor. He resided at 124 Pine Street, on the east side of the river, with his wife, Elizabeth, who died in 1925. In 1926 he remarried. In addition to serving as pastor, he worked as a handyman, mowing lawns and making small repairs around town. In 1925–1926 and 1927–1928 (from June to June of the years), Scott was replaced by Rev. J. C. McCrae, who resided with his wife, Anna, at 30 Elm Court, across from the church. And in 1929–1930, the pastor was E. H. Raynor, who resided in the rear of the church. Scott returned to the pastorate in July 1930.

On 13 August 1923 the trustees took out a new mortgage for $300 with the Great Barrington Savings Bank (Registry of Deeds, vol. 237, 62). Signing for the church were Jennie E. Moore, Mary Harrison, and Frederick L. Freeman. Jennie Moore was a longtime member and trustee who lived at 30 Elm Court. Fred Freeman was a laborer who lived at 37 Rosseter Street with his wife, Grace. Other members of the church were Edward Freeman, a woodchopper who lived on Hillside Avenue; Anderson Lewis, a teamster living at 130 Main Street; Harriet Williams, who boarded at 56 Taconic Avenue; Marion Billings; Henry Pickett; James L. Freeman; Charles Deas; and Lottie Watkins. The mortgage was paid off on 7 December 1928.

For most of the decade the activities of the church were by and large low-key and out of the public eye. With the opening of the Mahaiwe Theater on Castle Street in 1905, the churches, including the Clinton Church, had ceased to become major providers and venues for public entertainment. Nonetheless, the church continued its tradition of inviting outside pastors and speakers. In the summer of 1922 Mrs. Susan Murray from the New England Conference preached at the church for eight weeks. In September Rev. Ralph Paul Russell lectured and his three-year-old daughter, "Little Miss" Vera Russell, was among the singers. Delivering a lecture in November was the Rev. Thurston Chase of the Congregational Church; Rev. D. W. Thompson of Pittsfield gave one in December and again, the following year, in April. In addition, the usual church suppers, and ice cream and strawberry festivals continued to be organized by the women of the church.

On 11 August 1927 (p. 5), the *Courier* ran an interesting piece regarding two former members of the church:

Mrs. William Chinn of New York has loaned to the Mason Library a flute, the property of Thomas Jefferson McKinley, colored, who died in Great Barrington December 21, 1896. At the time of his death Mr. McKinley was the oldest resident of Berkshire county. Though the exact date of his birth is not known, it is the popular belief that he had seen a hundred and twelve summers. He was a vegetable and fruit dealer and was known to the people of his time as "Old Jeff." Though he was brought in bondage and uneducated, his intellectual vision was remarkably clear, and, in his rude way, he was somewhat of a philosopher.

Both the Chinns and McKinleys were early members of the church, and W. E. B. Du Bois was born in a cottage next to the McKinleys' house at the lower end of Church Street. The Chinns' daughter, May Edward Chinn, was one of the first Black women in the United States to become a physician and had a long career in New York City.

During the decade the church was also the locale for several marriages, and several longtime members died. Reverend Scott performed the marriage of several couples: Fred Freeman and Marion Billings on 4 April 1921; Henry Pickett and Bessie Hale on 2 December 1922; Anderson Lewis and Harriet Williams on 23 September 1923; and James Freeman and Eola Ormsby on 20 October 1928. George Jackson died at the age of fifty-seven on 27 February 1925. A lifelong resident of Great Barrington, he was a member of the first Children's Mite Society class in 1884. A month and a half later, on 12 April, the church lost trustee Jennie E. Moore at age seventy-one. She had been an early member of the church and a trustee for many years. Mrs. Jane Croslear of Sheffield died at the age of ninety-eight on 26 November 1927 and her funeral was at the church. The Croslears had been active in the several Black churches in Sheffield earlier in the century. On 5 April 1928 Mrs. Mary D. Harrison died and was buried in Elmwood Cemetery. The church lost William Battles on 17 August 1929. He lived with his wife Eliza at 135 Pine Street near Reverend Scott and was well known in town for his bootblack stand at the corner of Main and Railroad streets.

CHAPTER 5

Depression and War

The Great Depression and World War II were difficult years for the world, the United States, Great Barrington, and the Clinton Church. Nevertheless, these were two important decades for the Great Barrington African American community and the Clinton Church. During these years the Black community grew, stabilized, and became a more visible presence in Great Barrington. So, too, did the church, and perhaps more so than ever before, it became the heart of this African American group.

The Great Barrington African American Community in the 1930s and 1940s

As in the past, the African American community, compared with that of the white, was small, poor, and with little economic or political influence. But it was also growing, getting younger, localizing in one neighborhood, building new institutions of its own, and becoming more involved with the white community on equal or more nearly equal terms.

We know a good bit about the nature of the Great Barrington African American community from the 1930s up to the present, our knowledge coming from a mix of sources. In addition to considerable coverage in the *Berkshire Courier* and the listing of individuals in the southern Berkshire directories, we have the benefit of various church documents, including ledger books, membership rolls, and minute books of the church and its various organizations. These documents provide not just information but also a glimpse of the Great Barrington African American community and the church through the words of the members.

The records suggest that the annual population of African American adults and children in Great Barrington in the 1930s and 1940s ranged from about 125 to 150. The number of children is unknown, but it was surely more than in previous years and numbered about 25 including teenagers, at least 8 of whom were students in area high schools (Searles in Great Barrington and Williams in Stockbridge). The population varied by a few people from year to year, with a greater change in numbers from the winter to summer months each year. As had long been the case, the number of African Americans increased during the summer when some came to Great Barrington to work as cooks, maids, drivers, and laborers for wealthy, white, summer residents and tourist establishments. Some of these stayed on, and were the major source of the growing population.

Women made up the majority of the population, and about 50 percent of the women were single (widowed or never married). Reflecting the continuing systematic employment discrimination, nearly all were employed in unskilled or semiskilled jobs. Many men were laborers and women maids. Ried Cleaners on Main Street was probably the major employer of Blacks; being a presser was considered skilled labor for a Black man. Employment in the mills and town government was still closed. Among those who found skilled employment were Stephen Whittaker, who was a mechanic at Dempsey's garage on Railroad Street, and Pearl Whittaker, who worked for General Electric.

As in the time of Jason Cooley and Manuel Mason (mentioned in chapters one and three), there was some limited opportunity for Black entrepreneurs. In 1925 Albert and Susie Brinson opened the first dry-cleaning establishment in town after arriving from Georgia in 1922. Their store was in the Magadini block on south Main Street, and they lived with their children in an adjacent house. The business survived into the 1970s and counted the noted writer James Weldon Johnson, a summer resident of Great Barrington, among its regular customers. The most active Black entrepreneur of the 1940s was Martha Crawford, who lived with her husband, Isaac ("Ike"), and children at 14 Elm Court, across from the church. The family had moved to Great Barrington from Illinois in 1942. The house was a duplex, and Crawford used one side for her business ventures. She ran a tearoom in the house, later relocating it to the Magadini block; operated a summer employment agency for Blacks (Crawford Employment Bureau); offered lodging to Black travelers

(Crawford's Inn); and also had a catering service. In the late 1920s Edgar Willoughby and his wife, Minietta, ran the Sunset Inn, a lodging house and meeting facility for Blacks, on Rosseter Street, and in the 1930s he ran a tearoom on Castle Street where the Castle Street Café is now located.

During World War II several African American men from the southern Berkshires served in the military, including Joseph Gunn, Albert Brinson Jr., Elliot White, Isaac Crawford, Benjamin Carter, James Madison, Julian Hamilton, Bennie Carter, Clarence Gunn Jr., and Joseph Coffin. Clarence Gunn Jr. and Joseph Coffin had their photos in the *Courier,* as did many white servicemen. Across the United States, service by African American men in World War II (which was forced by African American leaders on a reluctant government) was a significant civil rights breakthrough and led to other civil rights advances of the following decades.

By the 1930s the streets around the church had become the Black neighborhood of Great Barrington. Many residents—although not all—of Elm Court, Rosseter Sreet, and Railroad Avenue behind the church were African American. Several African Americans also lived in homes near Rosseter Street on Main Street, on Castle Lane, and in two houses on lower Cottage Street. Because many of the homes housed two families and/or boarders, this small neighborhood was home to as many as four or five dozen African Americans of all ages. Those who lived outside the neighborhood were typically women working as maids and living in the homes of their employers. Localization around the church made African Americans a more visible minority in Great Barrington, in contrast with the dispersed minority they had been previously. Only a few church members lived beyond Great Barrington, such as former pastor Byron Scott, Charles Coffin (the former pastor of the Black church in Sheffield), and several members of the Gunn family in Stockbridge.

Relations with the White Community

Perhaps the most striking development of the 1930s and especially the 1940s was Blacks' greater involvement with and visibility in the Great Barrington community. The color line had surely not been broken, but contact with whites was more sustained and more equal than in the past. This involvement and visibility manifested themselves in various ways but were mainly social, religious, and educational; economic and political involvement remained minimal.

In March 1934 the Great Barrington Civic League sponsored a poetry reading at the Clinton Church. Church announcements begin to appear weekly in the "Church Announcements" column of the *Courier* in 1936, continuing into July 1938. On 10 April 1938 the church participated in a Union Palm Sunday service with the Methodist and Episcopal churches.

Another sign of Black and white interaction occurred in May 1938, when Anita Gunn, a 1937 graduate of Searles High School and a student at Petersburg Normal School in Virginia, died. (She was the daughter of Mr. and Mrs. Clarence Gunn of Rosseter Street.) The *Courier* noted on 12 May that "the members of the class of 1937 of Searles High school attended the funeral services in a body." Among other African American high school graduates during these decades were Eloise Brinson, Wray Gunn, Edna Wilks, Ruth Dove, Clarence Gunn Jr., Elaine Scott, Betty Gunn, and Vernon Croslear.

The most audacious crossing of the color line came in February 1943, when Reverend Morrison went before the selectmen to complain about the living conditions of African Americans. The *Courier* (15 February, 1, 4) reported his presentation at length:

> *Charges Negroes Are Ill-Housed Here*
> *Rev. H. W. Morrison Tells Selectmen of a Few Troubles*
> *Describes Some Houses as Unfit for Occupancy. Praises Board*
> *for its Impartial Attitude.*
>
> *Housing conditions for colored people in Great Barrington,*
> *the board of selectmen were told Monday night by Rev. Henry*
> *W. Morrison, are for the most part unfit for human habitation.*
> *Mr. Morrison, pastor of the A.M.E. Zion church for the past*
> *few years, and well known locally for his efforts on behalf of*
> *his parishioners, gave the board a plea for improvement in*
> *available housing facilities for his people.*
>
> *Mr. Morrison told the board that when the present war is*
> *over, America faces a new problem, which is involved with the*
> *general improvement in the national attitude towards people of*
> *different races and creeds.*

*He lauded the board for its past attitude of justice towards all
and the townspeople of Great Barrington in general, but brought
out that many of the "shacks" in which colored families are
forced to live here are breeding places of crime and disease.*

*The immediate cause for his appearance, he said, is the fact
that a local cleaning and pressing establishment has an exhaust
that sends constant noise and cleaning fluid odors into the
adjacent home of an elderly colored woman. He asked that the
condition be remedied, and while on the subject, asked that
the board investigate the conditions under which several other
colored families are forced to live. He described two localities
in town, the houses of which are poorly equipped, some having
constantly wet walls, while others lack the facilities for decent,
ordinary existence.*

*The board discussed Mr. Morrison's request, and decided that
either the board of health or the building inspector should be
notified of the conditions he reported.*

What came of his complaint is unknown. The individual suffering from
the exhaust fumes was most likely Rosa White, the Clinton organist, who
lived in the building at 9 Rosseter Street, behind Ried's cleaners.

The issue of Black-white relations was surely discussed by church members, and church records show two public discussions. In August 1944, on
a Thursday afternoon, the members heard a Mr. Sam Goodman: "Mr Sam
Goodman spoke on faith. Was very interesting. He was [unclear words] for
his feelings that the colored man should have equal rights and democracy"
(Clinton Church records). And on 30 December 1945 the minute book shows
that Rev. Green called a special meeting attended by Edward Watkins, Roberta Watkins, Jennie Freeman, Vernon Croslear, and Pinkie Brooks in which
"the discussion was how the white people feel towards the colored people as
a whole. There were few discussions and Rev. Greene spoke on some ideas
how to raise money for the church to pay Livingston College fee."

In the mid-1940s the church became more involved with other
churches and more visible as a religious institution. This was a time of
expansion for African American religion in Great Barrington, with the

People heading from buses to the Moorish Science Temple on south Main Street in the late 1940s. Source: Great Barrington Historical Society.

establishment of both the Macedonia Baptist Church and the Moorish Science Temple in 1944. The new church survived; the temple folded in 1949.

On 10 September 1944 the Clinton service was led by Reverend Ward of Monterey Church and twelve young people from his church, while in October 1945 Reverend Green was the speaker at the first fall meeting of the Congregational Guild. The Clinton Church also began to receive greater coverage in the *Courier*. In April 1946, for the first time in many years, an announcement of Clinton activities during Holy Week was provided in a page-one *Courier* article covering all churches in town. Such coverage continued for Easter and Christmas through May 1948. On 24 April 1947, for the first time, announcements for the Macedonia and Clinton churches began appearing in the "Coming Events" column of the *Courier*. And in 1948 and 1949 weekly announcements for the Clinton Church were published in the "Church Announcements" column.

The church also participated in joint services and other events with other Protestant churches in the region: in April 1946 Congregational minister Rev. Cornelius Nicholas Bakker was the speaker at evening services; in November 1947 there was a Union Thanksgiving Service with six other churches and the synagogue; in May 1948 the choir performed with seven other choirs at St. James church; and in November 1948 there was another Union Thanksgiving service at the Congregational Church.

Finally, on the social front, African American weddings began to get coverage equal to that of whites in 1949. Edna Dixon Hardy was the first Black bride to have her photo in the *Courier*, on 13 October 1949, announcing her marriage to Willie J. Wilks. Both worked for many years at Ried Cleaners, and Mrs. Wilks was superintendent of the Clinton Sunday school as well as a trustee board member and chair in the 1990s.

A report from the church to the Fourth Quarterly Conference in March 1944 reporting a donation for Livingston College. Source: Clinton A. M. E. Zion Church archives.

The Clinton Church 1930s–1940s

With the exception of a few years, the 1930s and 1940s were for the most part a period of growth and stability for the church. Several longtime members and pastors died during these years, but their numbers, and sometimes their work, were replaced by many new members, some of whom arrived from the South for summer employment and then stayed on. Among those who passed on were the following:

Nelson Piper at age 67 on 22 Dec 1930
Isaac W. Lewis at age 54 on 14 June 1931
Anderson Lewis (brother of Isaac) at age 58 on 6 July 1931
Allen Brooks at age 51 on 20 May 1934
Peter Joseph, son of Rev. Maurice T. Joseph, in car accident
    on 22 June 1934
Clarence Gunn, Robert Williams, and Mabel Walker Roister
    on 7 July 1938 (killed in car accident, with driver,
    Lester Waterman, critically injured)
Grace Freeman at age 79 on 4 February 1940
John Freeman at age 58 on 5 July 1942
Rev. Byron Scott, former pastor, at age 93 on 1 May 1944
Nancy Simms at age 65 on 13 Sept. 1944
Pearl Whittaker murdered in her home on Railroad Ave.
    on 6 May 1945
Rev. George Green, pastor, at age 76 on 8 June 1946

It was also a period of physical expansion for the church, with the parsonage completed in 1939, the church painted inside and out, the roof repaired, and new carpet laid, and in 1949 work began on converting the dirt basement into a meeting hall with a kitchen. An important legal development took place on 27 March 1945, when ownership of the property was transferred from the African Methodist Episcopal Zion Church of America to the Clinton Church. The national church had owned the property since 1914, when it had reclaimed it from the newly formed Second Congregational Church. Perhaps to prevent a recurrence of this type of transfer, the 1945 deed stipulated ". . . that no pastor nor trustee Board shall mortgage or sell any property of said Church without written consent of the Bishop of the District or the Annual Conference" (Registry of Deeds, vol. 277, 268).

Central to the stability of the church during these years was the multiyear service of several pastors:

I. B. Walters 1934–1936
Edward H. Coleman 1936–1940
Henry Morrison 1940–1945
Raleigh Dove 1946–1951

All four of these men worked hard to serve the membership and also to forge stronger ties with the Great Barrington community. Reverend Dove was especially active in the community and in pushing the church to raise money, keeping the building in good repair, and maintaining a harmonious membership. His daughter, Ruth D. Jones, worked as a cataloger at Simon's Rock College and was a leader of the 1968 and 1969 effort to create a national historic monument to W. E. B. Du Bois. The journal entry for 16 November 1947 in the church records aptly summarized his approach to the pastorate:

After the church service the pastor held a brief meeting at which
he thanked all members and friends of the church for their
splendid cooperation. He was encouraged by the work the church
was doing and pleaded for their continued help and interest.

S. Gunn (clerk)

Equally important to the work of the church were several active members. Among the women, the key contributors were Pinkie Brooks, Mary Jones, Rosa White, Hattie Dixon, and Roberta Watkins.

Wray Gunn remembers Pinkie Brooks as "a tough lady. She'd look you right in the eye and tell you where to go." Her toughness came from a conviction that she was doing the right thing, and she was an indefatigable worker for the church. Brooks's husband, Allen, died at the age of fifty-one in 1934. She lived at 183 Main Street (between what are now Brooks and the Caligari block) and raised her niece, Eloise Mitchell (Page) of South Carolina in her home. As a high school student, Mitchell ran the Sunday school. Brooks served as the church clerk, secretary of numerous societies, drove members to other churches and conferences, went door to door in town fund-raising, and did anything needed to keep the church going. She could also be counted to contribute extra money when necessary to pay the electricity bill or buy curtains for the parsonage. Her neatly organized and clearly written minutes of meetings and ledger books are a key source for this history.

Mary Jones was a quieter member, a regular attendee at services, and a steady contributor of no less than $1 each week and more when needed. Over the years she probably contributed more financially to the church than almost any other member. The usual weekly contribution was 25 or 50 cents, not the dollar she always gave. She worked as a maid for the Stevens family in their home on Main Street and lived at 30 Elm Court, in the building (now Berkshire Mountain Yoga) that also was home for Clinton members Nancy Simms, Ethel Wilson, and Lottie Wilson.

Employed as a maid and living at the rear of 9 Rosseter Street, Rosa White was the church organist and also organist for other groups in town. White came to Great Barrington at age sixteen from Camden, South Carolina, with her parents, Frank and Etta Reynolds, and her younger sister, Etta. Hattie Dixon and Pinkie Brooks were the primary contacts with the white community. Dixon lived at the rear of 27 Rosseter Street and was a first-rate organizer of fund-raising events. After the Macedonia Church was founded, she assisted with their events, although she remained a member of the Clinton Church. Roberta Watkins and her husband, Edward, were major fund-raisers and workers for the church in the late 1940s. Watkins was a laborer who worked for John B. Tracy, and the couple lived at 23 Rosseter Street.

Others who played key roles during these years were Charles Coffin, Fred Freeman, Charles Saunders, and Moses Haile. Fred Freeman was a laborer and lived at 4 Cottage Street. For many years until his death in 1950, he was the local preacher and conducted classes at the church and in Sheffield. In the early 1940s Charles Saunders also served as local preacher and played a key administrative role. He worked as a driver, and his wife, Wilhelmina, as a hairdresser, with a shop on Elm Court. They lived at 22 Elm Court and left the church to help found the Macedonia Church in 1944. Charles Coffin lived in Sheffield on Cook Road. At one time pastor of the Black church in Sheffield, he sometimes substituted for the Clinton pastor. Moses Haile became active in the church in the 1940s and resided, and still lives, at 32 Rosseter Street with his wife, Evelyn. In 2006 Haile, now an active ninety-five years old, was selected Rotary Person of the Year in Great Barrington. He had helped run the church and represented it in matters before the Great Barrington community. Also present and sometimes substituting for the pastor was former pastor Byron Scott.

Much of the work of the church, including the crucial task of raising funds, was carried out by its organizations, such as the Missionary Society, Poor Saints, Christian Endeavour, Sunday school, Choir, Trustee Board, Stewardess Board, and Youth Congress. During these years the church subscribed to the *Star of Zion, Church School Herald, Quarterly Review,* and *Missionary Seer.*

Unlike some previous years, by now the church was open year-round, with church attendance varying from summer to winter. Summer attendance ran from a dozen to thirty people, and in winter it dropped from sixteen to eight or so. More people attended Sunday evening services than morning services (rarely were men at the morning service, other than the pastor), and attendance was greatest on Easter, Christmas, Mother's Day, and the services on the day of quarterly meetings.

In June 1931 Rev. U. B. Bertrand arrived from Portland, Maine, to take over as pastor. The following year he was transferred to New London and replaced by Edward W. Gantt of Attleboro, Massachusetts, a graduate of Tyler and Paine colleges. An effort by the women to furnish his quarters was successful and led to the following notice being placed in the *Courier* (30 June 1932, 5): "The members of the Clinton A. M. E. Zion church wish to thank the friends who so kindly responded to the request for house furnishings, published in the *Courier* last week."

Although the Great Depression struck Great Barrington hard and left hundreds of people on government assistance, the Clinton Church finances actually stabilized in the 1930s. In 1933–1934 the Sunset Inn on Rosseter Street, run by Edgar Willoughby, was a major locale for church fund-raising events, and in August 1935 the church benefited from the performance of eminent dramatic reader Ada Bell Griffen. Further benefit—spiritual and financial—came from a five-day evangelical rally in September 1935, led by Rev. W. E. H. Lilly of Salisbury, North Carolina, and Rev. J. W. Platt of Waterbury, Connecticut, with services three times a day.

By January 1938 the church finances were in the best shape in years. In his "Third Quarterly Conference Report" in January, Reverend Coleman reported:

> *The financial condition of the church is good. All of the General Claims has [sic] been in on the 22nd of Nov $50.00. We thank God who has made all this accomplishment possible Standing Firmly upon the Foundation Faith, with our hands in Gods hands. With the everlasting light of hope beckoning us on we are ready to press forward trusting in Jesus Christ to gain the victory that life has for us. (Clinton church records)*

In March, things looked so good that he could slip a bit of bragging and favorable comparison into the "Fourth Quarterly Conference Report":

> *This year have been one of our achievement [sic] in Gt Barrington. Great Barrington was the first church in New England Conference to pay all her general claims. Gt Barrington led all churches in proportion in Livingstone College drive in the New England conference. We raised $10.50 over the amount we were appointed. The great Boston church raised 400 which was 26 percent of its general claims assessment. Gt Barrington raised $45.50 which was 91 percent of its general claims assessment. Boston 26 6/20 percent—Gt Barrington 91%. Gt Barrington have improved it church greatly this year. We have painted inside and outside and have laid new carpet and have paid for it all.*

Building the Parsonage

This set the stage for a successful effort to raise nearly $3,000 to build the parsonage on the rear of the church. The church clerk kept careful records of this activity, noting each contribution and each expense. The first income recorded is $101.11 on 9 August 1938. But real fund-raising did not begin until a year later, with nearly $2,500 raised between August and November 1939. In the end, $2,574.81 was raised from member contributions, fund-raising in town, and an anonymous gift of $1,847.85. Who the anonymous donor was remains unknown.

One possibility is Warren Davis, the only Black individual in town wealthy enough to do so.

Expense records begin with $12 for a blueprint on 15 August 1939 and end with $2.68 for thirteen pairs of curtains on 18 November 1939. The total cost was $2,756.41, with the overage made up by a loan of

One page from the church's expense report for 1945–46. Source: Clinton A. M. E. Zion Church archives.

$250 from member Edward Watkins. Watkins also worked on the construction and was paid $82.

The parsonage effort is well described by the pastor in his quarterly report (Clinton Church records):

> We have attempted a large program for the year having
> [inaugurated] a parsonage campaign seeking to raise $3000 the
> cost of a parsonage. The first effort have been made. The method
> of individual appeal through mail having been used. 3937 letters
> were sent out. The response not as well-been as deserved. Received
> $180.99. Paid out for printing and mailing $78.97. Balance in bank
> $102.02. (30 September 1938, Second Quarterly Conference)

> God heard our prayer and blessed us by touching the heart
> of one to help us and practically gave us our desire. Our
> membership struggled and sacrificed to great extent to help
> get this project started. We need to pause a while to meditate
> and give thanks to Almighty God. Let us continue to God's hand
> by faith and go on to higher heights. (19 October 1939, Second
> Quarterly Conference)

> Special Report to this quarterly conference. The am't raised and
> expended for the parsonage has been $2574. The parsonage is
> now complete. Our total $2,756.41. Balance $240.00 parsonage
> note. (30 December 1939, Third Quarterly Conference)

> This quarter has been one of the most eventful ones in the
> Church's history. Our much needed parsonage was completed
> and the pastor has been located here since Dec. 2. Bishop
> W. J. Walls visited us on Dec. 10 and the parsonage was
> formally dedicated. The financial report for this quarter is
> perhaps one of the largest in the history of the local church and
> perhaps exceeds that of any other church in the New England
> Conference. That report exceeds the sum of $2,794.43.

> We must acknowledge hard consistent labor of our small but very
> faithful membership that has been struggling to bear and to do

every task that I have set before them. We are thankful to God for
them. We are also very thankful for our unknown benefactor who
contributed $1,847.85 towards the erection of the parsonage.

As the old year draws to a close we can look back and see that
we have a firmer foundation to stand upon and more reasons
than ever before to give ourselves wholeheartedly upon the
Altar of Service to Almighty God. (30 December 1939, Third
Quarterly Conference)

The building of the parsonage was a key development in encouraging and
enabling pastors to remain with the church for several years. It meant
that the church could more easily pay their salaries and in addition freed
the pastors from performing other work to make a living. It also meant
that they could be more involved in the Great Barrington community; for
example, Reverend Dove (1946–1951) had three children who attended
the local schools. The "Fourth Quarterly Conference Report" in March
1940 shows the church valued at $6,000 and the parsonage at $3,000.

Decline and Growth in the 1940s

Perhaps the church overextended itself with the parsonage effort, since
it was soon burdened by several years of economic and membership decline. During these years Charles Saunders was very active in the church,
serving at times as a trustee, steward, "poor saint," preacher steward,
and local preacher. His wife, Wilhelmina, served for a time as clerk. Records for 1940 into 1943 are poorly kept and incomplete, and apparently
many quarterly conferences did not take place. This may have been because of a disagreement among members about payment of the conference claims. Saunders led the group that objected to paying the claims,
on the grounds that the Clinton Church could barely pay its own bills.
The majority evidently disagreed.

A report from 1 March 1942 shows the church in much debt: "debts $250
plus $375; general claims $35 balance out of $50 owed for year" (Clinton
Church records). The total raised in the last three quarters was only $428.16,
which was low compared with previous years when $170 to $200 was raised
each quarter. In addition, the church had to pay a one-time roof-repair bill of

$125. A year later, on 1 May, a report notes that the "membership [was] very small" and that the debt was $200, with $250 owed the pastor and $16.84 owed on general claims of $50.00 for the quarter.

In July 1943 the membership began a new effort to raise funds and pay off the debt. Through fund-raising rallies and suppers, by March 1944 they had raised $672.38, and in August Mrs. Pinkie Brooks led a major drive in the Great Barrington community. On 12 September 1944 she gave the church 500 fund-raising envelopes and that, combined with smaller amounts raised by other members, was used to pay off $324.36 in bills, leaving a balance of $40.40 in the treasury. The largest donor in town was Mrs. Blodgett, who gave $10, and the town's help was acknowledged in a letter to the *Courier* (21 September 1944, 4):

Editor Berkshire Courier:

The officers and members of the A.M.E. Zion church [wish] to thank everyone who helped on the church rally and mite box drive. It has been made possible through them that the committees can clear up all the back debts on the little church that stands at 9 Elm court. The amount raised was $324.36.

> *Rev. Henry W. Morrison, Pastor*
> *Edward Watkins, chairman*
> *Frank Reynolds, treasurer*
> *Mrs. Roberta Watkins, Chaplain*
> *Mrs. Pinkie Brooks, clerk*

Great Barrington
September 13, 1944

The church also sought new members and added fourteen over the next two years:

Mrs. Mary McArthur	Mrs. Sinclara Gunn
Mrs. Martha Sharpton	Mr. Ray M. Gunn
Miss Fannie Bell Donaldson	Mr. William H. Wooten

Mrs. Louise Ramsey
Mrs. Grace Smith
Mr. David Gunn Jr.
Wilheminia Reynolds

Frank Reynolds Jr.
Rosa Reynolds
Sammie Reynolds
Charles Smith

Several of these members—including Mrs. Sinclara Gunn and her son, Wray, and Frank and Wilheminia Reynolds—soon became active members. Mrs. Gunn took over as clerk in 1945 and began keeping a detailed journal book of the affairs of the church.

By the middle of 1945 the membership had rebounded, and the roll recorded for 8 June 1945 in the journal listed eighty-two current members, although not all were active or attended services. The journal also shows that from 1939 to 1962 the following children were baptized:

Barbara Verne Haile .... 21 February 1939
Moses Herbert Haile Jr............................... 7 June 1940
Deborah Diane Haile................................... 20 November 1941
Myrtle Austine Haile .... 26 October 1943
Harvey Henderson Haile .... 23 August 1945
Betty Jean McArthur................................... 1946
Alice Mary McArthur .... 17 April 1949
Rodney Smith.. 17 April 1949
Loretta Bowen .... no date
Dave Jones .... no date
George Reid Wilkes .... 3 April 1952
John Cochran .... 3 April 1952
Anthony Bowens .... 25 January 1953
Mary Ella Bowens .... 25 January 1953
Joan Dixon .... 4 October 1953
Leroy Smith... 6 October 1957
Terrell Perry.. 29 March 1959
Clarence S. Gunn III .... 27 December 1959
Gordon Scales .... 24 December 1961
Karl Ray Womble .... 14 January 1962
Allen McArthur .... 14 January 1962

At the urging of Reverend Morrison, the choir was reconstituted and counted among its members Marion Nelson, Moses Haile (secretary), Frank Reynolds (president), Willie Reynolds, Mrs. Morrison, Rosa White, Etta Reynolds (treasurer), Carrie Madison, Mattie Wilson, and Fannie Donaldson. Choir book minutes show that the organization was run strictly, with attendance at rehearsal mandatory and members fined ten cents when they were absent. Several social and fund-raising events (a silver tea at Pinkie Brooks's, a play in October, and a Christmas party for the children) rounded out the year, which saw the church with a balance of $83.23. And the pastor had been paid regularly from June 1944 to January 1945.

On 6 May 1945 the community was shocked when Pearl Whittaker was murdered by Willie E. Winn of Pittsfield, who fired a shotgun through the front door of her Railroad Avenue house, wounding her fatally in the chest and arms. Winn fled the area but was arrested in Cleveland, Ohio, the next week and brought back for trial. In January 1946 he pleaded guilty to second-degree murder and received a life sentence.

Fund-raising efforts continued, and by June 1945 the church had $1,096.96 in the bank, with the pastor now being paid regularly, usually $15 per week. In June Reverend Morrison had been replaced by Rev. George Green. The 30 September Women's Day/Missionary Day event raised $59.28, and on 8 November the ledger book (Clinton Church records) shows that "the ladies of Clinton A. M. E. Zion Church held a supper at Walker Hall and raised money to pay the Pastor's salary in the winter months when there are not many attendants at church." They raised $125.22. "Also Mrs. Jennie Freeman, Miss Mary Jones presented to the Parsonage 2 day beds to help with the furnishing of the Parsonage."

On 25 April 1946 Reverend Green married Mrs. Sadie Andergee David of Hyde Park, New York, in the parsonage, and then, less than two months later, on 9 June he died after a brief illness at Fairview Hospital at the age of seventy-six. Services were held at the church and officiated by the Congregational minister, after which his body was taken to New Haven, Connecticut, for another service and burial. Green had spent most of his career in Connecticut before coming to Great Barrington.

Reverend Green was replaced by Rev. Raleigh Dove, who lived in the parsonage with his wife, Minnie, and three of their children. Serving ably for the next five years, he was popular with the membership. In

The Easter program for 1946. Source: Clinton A. M. E. Zion Church archives.

```
                              EASTER PROGRAM
                              April 21, 1946

              Mrs. Pinkie Brooks-----Arrangement
              Mrs. David Gunn----Mistress of Ceremony

 1. Opening----- # 1---"T's Happy Easter"

 2. Scripture------Mrs. Charles Saunders

 3. Prayer-------Reverend Green

 4. Page # 3-----"Easter Prayer Response"

 5. Song # 4----"Easter Day Is Here"

 6. Reading------Mrs. Moses Haile

 7. Song # 6---"Angel of Easter Morning"

 8. Reading----Mrs. Frank Reynolds

 9. Offering--------Mr. Edward Watkins
    Gleaners--------Mr. David Gunn
    Song # 10--- "Crown The King of Glory"

10. Reading----Mrs. Otis Wilson

11. Song # 7----"In The Springtime"

12. Brief remarks by Reverend  Green

13. Song # 11----"Over The Years"

14. Something To Remember By-----Mrs. Brooks

15. Song # 9------"The Living Lord"

16. Reading-------Mrs/ Mary Mossie

17. Song # 12----"So Calm The Garden"

18. Few remarks by Elder Jackson

19. Closing song # 13------"Facing Forward"

20. Benediction---------Reverend Green
```

the quarterly conference before each New England Conference, Clinton members requested that he be returned to the church, which he was, until January 1951. In 1947 he initiated a mission to Sheffield. The mission was ended in April 1948 because of poor attendance, but resumed in 1950. His daughter, Ruth D. Jones (died 2005), worked at Simon's Rock College for many years and was active in the NAACP in the 1960s. She was also instrumental in the successful endeavor to have the W. E. B. Du Bois boyhood homesite on Route 23 designated a national historic site in 1969.

The Basement Meeting Hall

The decade closed where it began, with a major construction project. Because the church was small, most events had to be held in homes, public halls, or other churches, and the membership wanted a meeting place of their own. The work to convert the dirt-floored cellar to a basement meeting hall was initiated by Reverend Dove on 19 January 1947. The journal (Clinton Church records) recounts:

> *A membership meeting was held following the church service. The pastor expressed the desire for the church to raise $4,000 for the year. Part of which would go towards putting a basement in the cellar, so that the church might have a place for social gatherings. He also explained that because the new oil stove was not giving satisfactory heat, that the trustees had decided to take it down and put old coal stove back. The members were in accord with both.*

> *Respectfully submitted*
> *(Mrs.) Sinclara Gunn, clerk.*

The project was not a small one, since the basement had to be dug deeper, concrete poured, the ceiling reinforced, a bathroom and kitchen installed, and then the hall decorated and furnished. In addition, the kitchen needed a stove, cooking equipment and supplies, and service for guests.

On 2 March 1947 the members outlined a plan to raise the money, again reported in detail in the journal in an account that also sheds light on other aspects of the church's finances:

The moderator [Reverend Dove] *stated that he had in mind running two or three paid advertisements in the paper, to enlighten the public as to what the church was trying to do toward the building fund for the church. He was also asking aid of white friends. He had also been to the bank and secured*

THE CLINTON A. M. E. ZION CHURCH

GREAT BARRINGTON, MASS.

May 10, 1946

Mr.

Dear Mr. *Reh*

As you probably know, the Clinton A. M. E. Zion Church for a number of years stood for the Spiritual and Moral and Social uplift of our group of people in the town, but being small has not always been able to meet its financial obliga-
· tions.

While this year has been more or less a successful one with us, yet we find ourselves somewhat in need of funds to complete our budget for the year ending June 1st, 1946.

Believing that you are interested, we are asking you to help us at this time to raise THREE HUNDRED DOLLARS. The money is needed to meet some pressing obligations and to help in the work of the ministry.

Kindly send your contribution to our treasurer, Edward Watkins, 23 Rosseter Street, Great Barrington, Mass.

Acknowledging past favors and thanking you in advance for your kind consideration of this matter,

Yours very sincerely,

Edward Watkins, Treasurer

Pinkie Brooks, Clerk

Rev. George F. Green, Pastor

A fund-raising letter from May, 1946. Source: Clinton A. M. E. Zion Church archives.

another bank book to be used only for building fund. After a brief discussion the members voted to place one half of all funds (except those raised at regular church services) in bank for building fund, and the other half to go on book with the fund for the upkeep of church. The first money to be divided was proceeds from Baby contest, held Feb. 27 [$70.51].

After a brief discussion, the membership voted to pay Mrs. S. Gunn, clerk, and Mrs. R. White, organist, $2.00 each per mo. for their services. One member pointed out that this was not pay, but a gesture of appreciation.

Rev. Dove urged the members to attend church and these meetings so that they would know definitely what was going on in the church. He also hoped the church members would repay him the $50.00 he had paid for church claims in the near future. He felt that the church would do this in the near future [which it did on 6 April].

The meeting adjourned.
(Mrs.) S. Gunn, clerk.

The church proceeded with its plan, and the basement fund grew slowly from $81.17 in April 1947 to $276.94 in August, $482.31 in January 1948, and then $500.00 in July. In August 1948 the membership met again to discuss the basement.

The members of the church met for a few minutes at the church to discus the basement. Rev. Dove suggested that since the church did not have all the money would the church be willing to borrow it from the bank.

The estimated cost by a leading local contractor including painting the church inside and out around $3,000.
After a short discussion the church agreed.

A motion was made by Mrs. R. Freeman and seconded by Mr.
Petty that the church borrow the money. The motion carried.
Rev. Dove, Mr. Watkins and Mrs. S. Gunn were appointed to see
which bank would make the loan.

The meeting adjourned.
S. Gunn, clerk. (Clinton Church records)

Later in month Mrs. Gunn reported in the journal:

The church was unable to borrow the money from any bank, as no
one would sign for it. They therefore decided to build the basement,
with what they had, and with the churches own laborers.

And, in September 1948 work began:

Work on basement began, with free labor from volunteers and
Mr. McArthur acting as supervisor.

Fund-raising continued, and the men worked away over the next three
years. The rough work was finished in 1950 but was not fully completed
until September 1951. Although the church could now hold events in the
building, the basement never proved entirely satisfactory, since the floor
got wet when it rained, the ceiling was low, and the staircase was difficult
for elderly members. Suggestions that the church acquire an adjacent
building or add to the existing building never came to fruition.

The Local Preacher

An important position in the church was that of the local preacher, filled
in the 1930s and 1940s by Frederick A. Freeman and Charles Saunders.
As the following quote from the 30 March 1939 "Fourth Quarterly Conference Report" (Clinton Church records) indicates, it was a position that
required study, training, and approval of the church hierarchy:

Rev Coleman recommend Bro Chas R. Saunders for Local
Preacher license. But all person[s] applying for license has to

[obtain] Exhorter license first. It was motion by Bro Edward Watkins and second by Br. F. A. Freeman that Bro Chas R. Saunders receive Exhorter license. The Presiding Elder [Dr. H. R. Jackson] says that he have to be more careful in giving a license than he used to be. It calls for a very close examination.

Each quarterly report detailed the local preacher's activities, again for 30 March 1939:

Local Preachers Report

1 Numbers Sermons Preached 7
2   " "   Prayer Meetings held................. 2
3   " "   Class Meetings held................... 12
4   " "   Times Attended S School............ 13
5   " "   Funerals Conducted.................. sealed
6 What service he has rendered the Pastor.
  What soever service I have been able to give him.
7 What service he has rendered the Presiding Elder.
  Help to raise his assessment.
  What studies he is pursuing.
  The Bible. Church discipline.
  The Power of Pentecost — A. D. L. Moody
  Centenary Edition and the Renewal of a dead church [—] Moody

Bro F. A. Freeman[,] Local Preacher

In the southern Berkshires the local preacher also served the Sheffield Black community. The report for the Second Quarterly Conference on 19 October 1939 indicates that this service was extensive:

Report of Sheffield

No. of pastoral visits made 45
* " "   marriages performed........................ sealed*
* " "   funerals conducted .... " "*
* " "   baptized.. " "*

" " sermons preached............................. 15
S.S. organized with 12 pupils
No. of conversions 7
" " received on probation 7
" " of probationers rec'd
into full membership..................... none
No. of members received
on certificate.................................... sealed
" " certificates granted............................ " "
No. withdrawn without certificate .... " "
No. expelled.. " "
No. of deaths .... " "
present number of probationers.................. 7
present number of full members .... sealed
Increase over last quarter........................... sealed

Benevolence Collections
1. For Distric[t] School................................ $2.00
2. " " Benevolence 5.00
3. " " General Claims 2.51
4. Subscribers to Our Periodicals
    1. Star of Zion
    2. Church School Herald Journal
    3. Quarter Review
    4. Missionary Seer

F. A. Freeman
Pastor in Charge

Social Clubs

In the 1940s two African American social clubs were founded in the
southern Berkshires. The first was the Progressive Club, established on
23 February 1944 at Beatrice Barboza's home in Stockbridge. The club
was a social and charitable organization for African American women in
the southern Berkshires. Some members were members of the Clinton
Church, others were not, and the club had no formal ties to the church,

although it sometimes donated money to the church, such as that for the basement fund in 1949. The founding members were as follows:

Mrs. Beatrice Barboza .... President
Mrs. Evelyn Haile .... Vice President
Mrs. Pearl Brinson .... Secretary
Mrs. Pinkie Brooks .... Treasurer
Mrs. Henry Morrison .... Chaplain
Mrs. Mary Mossie .... Social Committee
Mrs. Carrie Madison .... Social Committee
Mrs. Florence Gunn
Mrs. Edna Reid
Mrs. Charles Saunders
Miss Mabel Gunn
Mrs. Florence Gunn
Mrs. Minietta Willoughby
Mrs. Mattie Bowen

Dues were set at 20 cents a week divided equally between "social activities" and "club treasury," and some members regularly gave more. The club raised additional funds through suppers, its annual dance (beginning in 1945), and raffles. It gave teas at members' homes or Mrs.

Announcement of a Progressive Club dinner in 1946. Source: Clinton A. M. E. Zion Church archives.

116

PROGRESSIVE CLUB
presents its

"ANNUAL DANCE"

AT THE SEARLES AUDITORIUM
Bridge Street, Great Barrington, Mass.

THURSDAY EVENING, AUGUST 4, 1949

Music By BOB BEVERLEY AND HIS BAND

Subscription—including tax—$1.25

Ice Cold Soda For Sale   9:00 P. M. to 1:00 A. M.

A Progressive Club dance ticket from 1949. Source: Clinton A. M. E. Zion Church archives.

Crawford's tearoom, held parties for adults and children, gave money to servicemen, bought Christmas presents for children, made donations to orphanages, and gave scholarship money to local college students.

On 6 November 1948 the Jolly Club #12 was founded. The club's minute book records that "the Jolly #12 Club [was] organized by Mrs. Pinkie Brooks as a social entertainment club to have social interaction on Saturday nights" (Clinton Church records). The fifteen founding members were the following:

Mrs. Brooks .... Great Barrington
Mrs. Brown .... New York City
Mr. Brown .... New York City
Miss Cook .... Lee, MA
Mr. Dockett .... Boston
Mrs. Gunn .... Great Barrington
Mrs. Hamilton .... Great Barrington
Mr. Hamilton .... Great Barrington
Mrs. Hill .... Great Barrington
Mr. Hill .... Great Barrington
Miss Mitchell .... Great Barrington
Mrs. Johnson .... Risingdale, MA
Mr. Johnson .... Risingdale
Mr. Pittman .... Roxbury, MA
Mr. Whittaker .... Great Barrington

Mr. Johnson was the first president, Mrs. Hamilton the vice president, and Mrs. Brooks the secretary. As in the Progressive Club, dues were collected at weekly meetings held in members' homes, although the activities of the club seemed more purely social with card and game parties, and dinners for the members. The minute book for 1948 reports the following dinner:

> *Nov 5. Club dinner held at Mrs. Julian Hamilton house 118 Main St. The menu consist[ed] of broiled chicken, peas, escalloped potatoes, pork chops, rolls, butter, peanuts, candy, ice cream, apple pie, tea, coffee, soda. Favors were given to each one. Games played. There 11 members present. It was an enjoyable evening. Next meeting be at Mrs. Gunn.*

The club disbanded on 15 December 1951, with the treasury distributed among the members, each receiving $12.78, although the club apparently was revived in the 1970s.

New African American Religious Organizations in Great Barrington

The size and stability of the Great Barrington African American community was certainly one consideration in the establishment of two additional African American religious bodies in the 1940s.

Movement toward the formation of a Macedonia Baptist Church in Great Barrington evidently began in the summer of 1944. The record of the August Conference Report (Clinton Church records) shows Charles Saunders "planning to resign from all offices[;] also left the AME Zion Church for being dissatisfied." According to Wray Gunn, the dissatisfaction refers to a disagreement among the membership over payment of claims to the New England Conference. Some, like Saunders, argued that since the Clinton Church had trouble paying its own bills, the church's paying claims to the national church was not fair. The Macedonia Baptist Church, which had established a missionary effort in town, required no contribution to a central organization and thus provided an economic alternative. Charles and Wilhemina Saunders and Martha and Isaac Crawford were founding members of the Macedonia Church, which met at first in the Crawford home at 14 Elm Court across from the Zion Church.

Relations between the members of the two churches were evidently friendly from the beginning. Mr. Saunders's resignation from the Zion Church was noted in the minutes (Clinton Church records):

Motion by Mrs. Watkins second by Mr. Watkins that Mr. Saunders resignation be accepted from all offices of the Church also sever his membership from AME Zion Church. It was accepted with regret. After which Rev. Morrison gave a little talk and pray that God bless him, on his journey that he is beginning to take up.

On 17 September a ledger entry notes that "Mrs. Charles Saunders from Macedonia Baptist Mission sang two solos" ("Take My Hand Precious Lord, Lead Me On" and "Just a Closer Walk with Thee") at the funeral of Nancy Simms on 15 September. In 1946 the two churches held joint services during Holy Week, alternating between the two meeting places, with Reverend Green presiding at most services. On Sunday morning the women of the Zion Church provided breakfast for members of both churches. Mrs. Hattie Dixon, an active member of the Zion (Clinton) Church and an important link with the white community, assisted the Macedonia Church with fund-raising activities, and in January 1949 Macedonia pastor Robert Harrell was guest pastor at the Zion Church. Relations between the two churches have remained cordial over the years, with regular sharing of the pulpits and joint services.

The first full-time pastor of the Macedonia Church was Rev. Robert Harrell who came from the Zion Baptist Church in Waterbury, Connecticut. He was installed on 27 July 1947. The Macedonia Church was Great Barrington's second African American Church, meeting in members' homes and public halls until it moved into its own building at 9 Rosseter Street in 1955. The Clinton Church sees itself as the mother church of the Macedonia Church.

The year 1944 also marked the arrival of the Moorish Science Temple in Great Barrington. Its presence in Great Barrington was much shorter-lived and more contentious than were the other two churches. On 24 September 1944 the Clinton Church had perhaps the most interesting of the many guests at worship services over the years. The guests are recorded in the attendance book as "The Princess Heshla Amanda Tamanya from Abissinia" and "The Grand Sheik Frederick Turnel of Morrocco." The latter was Grand Sheik S. Frederick Turner-el, the leader of the Moorish Science Temple Divine and National Movement of North America; the princess was his wife. They were in town to purchase property for the establishment of a Moorish Science Temple and a school. According to church records Turner-el spoke at the afternoon service: "There was a service at 3 o'clock. The Rev. Turnel of Morrocco spoke to us. He gave a very good lecture. The Princess was unable to sing as she had a very bad throat and cold."

Moorish Science Temple Divine and National Movement of North America was one of two major surviving sects of the Moorish Science Temple founded by Noble Drew Ali (Timothy Drew) in the early twentieth century. The movement taught that African Americans were of Middle Eastern rather than African descent and that Islam was their true religion. To mark their Middle Eastern identity, men wore fezzes and robes and added *el* or *bey* to their names. When Ali died in 1920, the movement divided into several subgroups.

In November 1944 the Temple agreed to purchase the Lord Barrington Hotel on south Main Street (located on the lot where Guido's is now located) as its headquarters and also to purchase the 300-acre Brush Hill farm in Sheffield. The hotel was purchased from Lucille and Frank Stanton and the farm from Mrs. Stanton's brothers, Earl and Morrison Jones in December 1945. Although envisioned as sect headquarters, the building seems not to have been fully used in the four years of occupation by the Temple. Evidently only a few members were ever in permanent residence, but it was used for services attended by members from elsewhere and for occasional social events. Attendees often arrived on charter buses. Wray Gunn recalls that it drew little interest in the local African American community, although he and other youths would skate on the skating rink in the winter.

Relations between the Temple officials and the town were largely difficult. Despite tax-board rulings to the contrary, the church resisted paying taxes as a religious organization, objected to the tax rate, and filed a racial and religious discrimination claim with the governor's office. In addition the Temple had trouble paying off the mortgage to Mrs. Stanton, and a lawsuit for foreclosure brought in November 1948 led to the Moorish Temple leaving the property in July 1949. The sheik issued an apology to the town, saying he had been misinformed when he claimed the tax policy was motivated by racism and religious prejudice.

CHAPTER 6

Civil Rights and Social Activism

The 1950s into the 1970s was a time of enormous significance for African Americans in particular and American society in general. In 1954 in *Brown v. Board of Education of Topeka, Kansas,* the Supreme Court ruled unanimously against school segregation, overturning its 1896 decision supporting the "separate but equal" doctrine of *Plessy v. Ferguson.* In the following year the Montgomery Bus Boycott began and continued into 1956, marking the beginning of the civil rights movement. More than 200,000 people participated in the March on Washington in 1963, and civil rights leader, scholar, Great Barrington native, and A. M. E. Zion participant W. E. B. Du Bois died in that year in Ghana, where was buried. Du Bois's wife, Nina Gomer Du Bois, had died in 1950 and was buried in Mahaiwe Cemetery, in Great Barrington, next to their infant son. In 1964 the Civil Rights Act became law, and in 1968 civil rights leader Rev. Martin Luther King Jr. was assassinated, precipitating race riots in several cities.

None of this was lost on the Berkshire African American community, and local developments mirrored national ones. In 1945 the Berkshire chapter of the NAACP (established in 1918) became active again, and in 1960 and again in 1963 organized protests at Woolworth's in Pittsfield, Massachusetts. The following year Reverend King Jr. lectured at Williams College, in Williamstown, Massachusetts. Race relations soured in Great Barrington in 1968. There was a very public controversy, continuing into the fall of 1969, over the establishment of a memorial for Du Bois at his boyhood home on Route 23. There were also charges of police harassment of Black youths, which eventually found Reverend Durante of the

Clinton Church leading a townwide committee to find common ground in police relations. In 1969, after several years of hard work and much controversy, the W. E. B. Du Bois boyhood homesite on Route 23 in Great Barrington was dedicated as the W. E. B. Du Bois Memorial Park.

For the Clinton Church these decades were a period of both stability and change. Greater involvement by church members and the African American community in general in white society, a trend that had begun in the 1930s, continued. We see evidence of that trend in three weddings in 1951 in three different churches in town. On Easter Sunday, 25 March, Elaine Scott married Clarence Gunn Jr. at the Clinton Church. On 10 June Betty E. Gunn married Kenneth E. Cottman of Delaware at St. James Episcopal Church, and on 30 June Eloise Brinson married William L. Woods of West Virginia at the United Methodist Church. Not insignificant was that five of the six newlyweds were college students or recent graduates. By the early 1970s, integration was moving forward. There were several Black teachers in the public schools. A Black Studies course was offered at Monument Mountain Regional High School. Wray Gunn, chair of the Trustee Board of the church was also president of Construct, Inc., the not-for-profit housing agency. Moses Haile was president of the Lion's Club in 1974, and Wray Gunn in 1975. Young Black women were sponsored each year in the Laurel Festival Queen contest. A Black police officer, Ralph C. Moddy Jr., was hired on the force for the first time in Great Barrington. Rick Lawrence of Great Barrington, sponsored by the Southern Berkshire American Legion Post #127, was elected governor of Boy's State. In 1974 Wayne Gunn, son of Clinton trustee Wray Gunn and sponsored by Sheffield American Legion Post #340, was also elected governor of Boy's State. And he was the president of the Mount Everett Regional High School class of 1975.

Years of Growth: 1950–1953

The decade was only a little over seven months old when Clinton Church lost Frederick Freeman at the age of 63 on 7 August. A resident of 4 Cottage Street, he was the son of Frederick and Grace (Crossley) Freeman of Sheffield and left behind his wife, Jennie; one brother; and two sisters. Frederick Freeman, a longtime active member of the church, served as local preacher, taught religion classes, ran the mission to Sheffield, and substituted for the pastor on several occasions. His death followed by only a month the mysteri-

DISTRICT CONFERENCE PROGRAM

HARTFORD DISTRICT OF THE NEW ENGLAND
CONFERENCE, CHURCH SCHOOL AND CHRISTIAN
ENDEAVOR, WOMEN'S HOME AND FOREIGN
MISSIONARY, AND HOME MISSION MASS MEETING

at

THE A. M. E. ZION CHURCH

Great Barrington, Massachusetts

Wednesday, Thursday and Friday

September 26th, 27th, 28th, 1951

Rt. Rev. William Jacob Walls, A.M., D.D., *Presiding Bishop*
Rev. H. B. Norville, *Presiding Elder*
Rev. J. C Johnson, *Pastor*

DISTRICT AND CONFERENCE MISSIONARY AND

CHRISTIAN EDUCATION OFFICERS

Each Minister is asked to Register One Delegate from each
Church School, One from the Christian Endeavor, and One
from the W. H. F. M. Society.

Registration—$10.00 Per Person for the Three Day Period.

All Local Elders, Deacons, Exhorters, Superanuated and
Missionary Evangelists are expected to Register—$3.00.

MISSIONARY DISTRICT OFFICERS

Mrs. Josephine Morris, *District President*
Mrs. Cornelia Parks, *Secretary of Y's*
Mrs. Naomi Mims, *Sup't. of Buds*
Mrs. Inez Jefferson, *Pres. Life Members Council*
Mrs. M. L. McDew, *District Supply Captain*

HOME MISSIONS

Mrs. Arrelia Weston, *President*

CHRISTIAN EDUCATION OFFICERS

Mrs. Jeanette English, *Conference Director*
Mrs. Francis Green, *Director of Adults*
Mr. Wm. Hooker, *Director of Youth*
Mrs. Laura Bellamy, *Director of Children*

Cover of the program for the District Conference Program held at the church in
September 1951. Source: Clinton A. M. E. Zion Church archives.

ous death of Albert Brinson, age 26, who died in a hit and run accident while walking home from work early in the morning on South Egremont Road.

The Clinton members noted Freeman's meaning to the church in a memorial placed in the journal on 13 August 1950 (Clinton Church records):

Rev. Frederick Freeman (deceased)

On Monday, Aug. 7, 1950, a voice from Heaven gently whispered, Rev. Freeman, you have finished "Your work on earth, come up higher."

Since the dawn of creation the penalty of life has been death, and yet with this knowledge it is hard to understand why one who has given his life preaching the word of God should be stricken, but they go, and we beseech thee O Lord, to remind us Thy Will be done.

Rev. Freeman was devoted to the church he loved so well, and his passing has left a great vacancy in the church and community.

He walked with us down life's good way but left us at the gate that opens outward whose portals he must pass above.

The members of Clinton A. M. E. Zion Church extend their deepest sympathy to the bereaved family, and resolve that a copy of these resolutions be given the family, and one spread one the church records.

Sleep on Rev. Freeman and take your rest.

The members of the church and your family loved you, but God loves you best.

From the officers & members of Clinton A. M. E. Zion Church.

Rev. R. Dove   Pastor
Mrs. S. Gunn   Clerk

ORDER OF RELIGIOUS SERVICES

Clinton A. M. E. Zion Church

Great Barrington, Massachusetts

REV. A. W. JOHNSON, Minister

1. Organ Prelude
2. Processional and Doxology
3. Pastorial Prayer
4. Hymn
5. Responsive Reading

THE CREED

I believe in God, the Father Almighty, maker of heaven and earth; and in Jesus Christ, his only Son, our Lord; who was conceived by the Holy Ghost, born of the Virgin Mary; suffered under Pontius Pilate; was crucified, dead and buried; the third day he arose again from the dead. He ascended into heaven and sitteth at the right hand of God, the Father Almighty; from thence he shall come to judge the quick and the dead. I believe in the Holy Ghost; the holy Catholic Church; the communion of saints; the forgiveness of sins; the resurrection of the body; and life everlasting. *Amen.*

6. Gloria Patri
7. Scripture
8. Prayer
9. Charity Offering
10. Notices
11. Hymn
12. Sermon
13. Invitation Song
14. Offering
15. Recessional and Doxology
16. Benediction

Order of Religious Services in 1951—52. Source: Clinton A. M. E. Zion Church archives.

On 14 January 1951 Reverend Dove surprised those gathered at the quarterly meeting when he announced his departure: "Rev. Dove in a few remarks stated that as this was his last meeting held here, he wished again to thank the membership for their cooperation. He hoped the church would continue to prosper. He had been wonderfully blessed while here. The people had been good to him" (Clinton Church records).

Leaving in the middle of the conference year was unusual, since ministerial changes were typically announced at the May district conference, with the new pastor taking over in June or July. Reverend Dove was popular in the church and the Great Barrington community. His three youngest children attended school there, and a photo in the 6 April 1950 edition of the *Berkshire Courier* shows that the William Cullen Bryant school varsity and junior varsity basketball teams, which won league titles, includes Reverend Dove's son, Jesse; Everett Brinson; and LeBaron Stallon. There is nothing in the church records to suggest any issues with Dove; in fact he returned as a guest preacher in February 1952. He moved to Worcester, Massachusetts, and later to Brooklyn, New York, but returned to town with his wife to visit often, since their daughter Ruth lived on Castle Lane with her husband, David Jones (Ruth later worked as a cataloger in the library at Simon's Rock College). Reverend Dove died in Brooklyn in May 1962.

Dove's replacement was Rev. Luther A. Halloway, who had been a guest preacher the previous September. Perhaps Reverend Dove was seen by the district as a less than fully engaged administrator, because Reverend Holloway immediately began to reorganize the church with the support of the district presiding elder, Reverend Norvell. A 14 February 1951 journal entry (Clinton Church records) notes:

> *Rev. Holloway stated that the purpose of the meeting was to get the church organization before him; to acquaint himself with the officers and members of the auxilliaries; to hear their financial reports, thereby ascertaining the financial status of the church.*

And a 15 April quarterly conference report notes:

> *In his closing remarks, Rev. Norvell said that Rev. Dove had labored hard here, and had left the church in good condition,*

materially, financially and spiritually. He also left with a high
standing in the community. Much can be said of his good work.
Now, we are the same people, and the same church, all working
for the same one God, and he was sure that these people of
the layety would give Rev. Holloway the same cooperation
regardless of changes, so that the church would go on to higher
and nobler deeds and acts of love (Clinton Church records).

In June Reverend Holloway was replaced by Rev. Alexander Johnson, who relocated from Elizabeth City, North Carolina:

The Minister then proceeded with the business. He greeted the
people, stating that he was a stranger, not only to the people,
but to the conference also. He was glad to be sent to Clinton, and
would do his best to keep the church going forward. His biggest
problem was getting his family here. He was staying at Mrs.
Watkins and paying some rent to her and board at restaurants,
so he was anxious to get his family here, because he was having
to support two familys when they are separate. (Clinton Church
records, journal entry, 19 June 1951).

A divided membership voted to provide Reverend Johnson with $200 to help his family move to town. He remained pastor until 1954, when he was transferred to Providence, Rhode Island, and replaced by Rev. David Woodson. Johnson had been a popular leader, and he and his wife had been honored by the membership in January 1953 on their twenty-fifth wedding anniversary with a silver tea set. His popularity is evident in a story told by his daughter, Mrs. Mary Bridgemahon, of Meriden, Connecticut, at a gathering at the Clinton Church in September 2005. Mrs. Bridgemahon recalled that in 1954 the members feared that Bishop Walls would reassign her father to another church. So they rented a bus and attended the conference to make their wishes known. Bishop Walls, knowing what they were up to, made her father's appointment to Providence the last one of the day and then quickly exited into his office.

Finishing the Basement and the District Conference

Two noteworthy developments in 1951 went hand in hand. One was the completion of the basement dining hall, the other the convening of the district conference at the church in September. The looming conference was the driving force in getting the basement completed. It was a difficult project because it required much work and much money, which had to be raised in the absence of bank financing. Through the end of 1950 the church had spent $1,566 on the basement and had raised $1,645.59. Major sources were Mrs. Rachel Freeman's pot soliciting ($202.37), Mrs. Dixon's turkey dinner ($153.75), an April 1949 rally ($93.17), an August 1949 Stewardess Board rally ($148.30), and Reverend Dove's August 1949 rally ($90). (Mrs. Freeman's pot soliciting was her practice each spring of setting up a Salvation Army–style pot on the corner of Bridge and Main streets to collect money for the church.) In 1951 the church raised $110.51 from a white sale and additional sums from a rally, turkey suppers, and a bazaar. And, in a final flurry of fund-raising, in September 1951, members gave money and many items to finish the basement and have it ready for the conference: dishes, silverware, table covers, towels, cleaning supplies, and food, as well as lodging for visitors. Mrs. Roberta Watkins and the Stewardess Board raised money to have a bathroom moved upstairs at a cost of $554.46.

A 15 July 1951 journal entry was the first mention of the district conference:

In the absence of Rev. Johnson at the last check up meeting, Rev. Norvell said he had invited the district conference to convene in Gt. Barrington, Sept. 26–28. He felt that it would be a big help to the church, and would let the people know just who was behind the church. The members discussed the matter pro and con. The main issue being the unfinished basement. The members were assured that if later they found they were unable to entertain the conference, Rev. Morris at Hartford would. A motion was made by Mrs. Wilks seconded by Mrs. Watkins that Clinton Zion Church entertain conf. Motion carried.

Rev. David Woodson and church members in the mid-1950s. Source: Clinton A. M. E. Zion Church archives.

A week later the members went to work: "The members were reminded that the church had agreed to entertain the district conference Sept. 26–28. The members seemed very enthusiastic about the affair, and many expressed the wish to get ready, to go to work and get prepared. Mrs. Watkins stated that she and Mrs. Freeman would contact the furniture store again about the stove, sink and hot water heater for basement kitchen" (Clinton Church records, journal entry, 23 July 1951).

Taking place from September 26 to 28, the conference brought several dozen people to town. The journal entry for 30 September commented:

Presiding Elder Norvell was present during all sessions. It was a joyous time in Great Barrington during all of the services. They all enjoyed the Great Barrington hospitality to the utmost. Their food was good. Moneys raised from registration and food went to Clinton A M E Zion Church. Total raised at conference was 181.76. Expenses of food, printing, cook, soda and the ice

133.90. Paid all expenses and the balance $47.86 was turned over to church treasurer Miss Reynolds. There was happiness in all corners of church at this meeting.

Unfortunately, a fire on 4 November caused $500 damage to the basement ceiling and walls of the basement kitchen. Caused by over-heating in a stovepipe, it was put out by the fire department, and the losses were covered partially by insurance. On 31 December 1954 the basement suffered a second fire during the Watch Night Meeting. The flames and smoke damaged the women's bathroom and a wall of the parsonage living room. Insurance paid $608.75, and the damage was repaired.

From 24 June 1951 to 6 January 1952, the church raised $4,623.99. On 2 March 1952 the basement was dedicated and new items put into use. Among these (and their donors) were the following:

Silver bowl and plate (Mrs. Brooks and Mary Jones)
Pewter pitcher for sacrament wine (Mrs. Hattie Dixon)
Painting of Christ and lambs knocking on door in honor
  of Mrs. Rachel Freeman (Mr. Petty)
Easter scenery for pulpit (Sunday school)
Communion set (Mrs. Sauer)
Candleholders for pulpit (Mrs. Pinkie Brooks)
One dozen linen dish towels (Mrs. Marie Johnson)
Coffee urn (Missionary Society)
Two sets of big cooking pots (Missionary Society)
Ashtrays (Mr. and Mrs. Kennedy)
Rug for kitchen (Mrs. Brooks)
Twelve salt and pepper shakers (Mrs. Brooks)
Dining room table (Mabel Gunn)
Chairs and dining room table (Mrs. Hattie Dixon)
Thirty candles (Mrs. Brooks)

More Renovation and Possible Expansion

During the last five years of the 1960s and first four of the 1970s, a major attempt was made to raise the funds needed to renovate, maintain, and expand the church building. Leading the effort was Trustee Board chairman Wray Gunn of Sheffield. In March 1966 the downstairs kitchen was renovated, a new hot water heater installed, and new tables purchased for the dining room. This work was paid for with dinners, luncheons, and bazaars as well as weekly collections for the building and kitchen funds. These funds were also used to help pay the gas, hot water, and electric bills. In addition, a loan was obtained from the First Agricultural Bank of Great Barrington for $672 in March 1965 and paid off in December 1967, three months before it was due. In July 1969 the church borrowed another $1,300 from Agricultural National Bank for a new roof.

At the same time, a pledge letter was sent to the members by Gunn explaining long-term plans for new siding and insulation and a new room on the front, which might cost as much as $10,000. The purpose of the new room was to add meeting space that improved on the basement with its low ceiling and its wet floor when it rained. Members signed the pledge forms, and by December 1969 the fund enjoyed a balance of $432.70. Raising money to pay for the expansion was a primary activity of the first years of the 1970s. Funds were acquired through offerings, the pledges made by the members, fund-raising events such as the annual barbecue each August, church suppers, and donations from the community. Major community contributors included the United Methodist and St. James churches, Wheeler & Taylor, Chauncy Loomis Sr. of Stockbridge, Mr. and Mrs. Cornelius Johnson, and William Woods of Meriden, Connecticut. Mr. Woods was the husband of the former Eloise Brinson (died 2005), who had grown up in Great Barrington, her parents having opened Brinson's Cleaners in 1925. The church also set up memorial funds for Mary McArthur, Rev. Raleigh Dove, Grace Zinnermon, Albert Brinson, and Hattie Dixon, and donations to those funds were allocated to the building fund.

By August 1972 the church had plans drawn up for the expansion and obtained a bid, which was shown to the presiding elder. In November 1974 Presiding Elder Warren Brown noted that the building was in need of repair and asked that fund-raising be speeded up and the fund used to "get going to improve the Church" rather than to add an addition. According to the quarterly conference report (Clinton Church records), the "general opinion of those present is to get going." By September 1975 the building fund account had grown to $5,723.31, and the church renovation was begun. The covered porch was added to the front, new windows installed, and paneling placed on the walls. A story and photo in the *Courier* detailed progress as of November.

Membership

The late 1940s and early 1950s constituted a period of growth for the church; in 1952 there were sixty-six adult members, about a dozen children, and three Watch Care members.

1952 Membership

Bowen, Mrs. Mattie
Bowen, Mr. Willie
Bowlin, Mrs. L. (Lenox, MA)
Brinson, Mrs. Susie
Brooks, Mrs. Pinkie
Card, Mrs. Agnes
Cochran, Mr. John
Cochran, Mrs. Martha
  (Canaan, CT)
Coffin, Mr. Charles
Coffin, Mrs. Edith
Darling, Mrs. Alice
Davis, Mrs. Hattie
Dean, Mr. Selvern
Dixon, Mr. George, Jr.
Dixon, Mrs. Hattie
Freeman, Mrs. Jennie
Freeman, Mrs. Rachel
George, Mrs. Gertrude

Gunn, Mr. Clarence, Jr.
Gunn, Mr. David
Gunn, Mr. Ray Martin
Gunn, Mr. Saint Clair
Gunn, Mrs. Florence
Gunn, Mrs. Sinclara
Hamilton, Mrs. Zelene
Henderson, Mrs. Louise
Hill, Mr. Charles
Hill, Mrs. Hazel
Holder, Miss E. B.
Howard, Mr. Gus
Jaynes, Mrs. Leona (Lee, MA)
Johnson, Mrs. Marie S.
  (Risingdale, MA)
Johnson, Mrs. Mary
Johnson, Rev. A. W.
Jones, Miss Essie
Jones, Miss Mary

Jones, Mr. David
Jones, Mrs. Ruth
Kennedy, Mr. E. I.
Kennedy, Mrs. Barbara
Lewis, Mr. Joe
McArthur, Mr. Joseph Sr. (Pittsfield)
McArthur, Mrs. Katherine
(Pittsfield)
McArthur, Mrs. Mary
Moore, Mrs. Alice
(Great Neck, NY)
Petty, Mr. D. R.
Petty, Mrs. Inez
Reynolds, Mrs. Etta
Simmons, Mrs. Ossie Cook
Smith, Mr. Charlie
Smith, Mrs. Fanny
Smith, Mrs. Grace (Lenox)
Walton, Mrs. Emma
Watkins, Mr. Edward
Watkins, Mrs. Roberta
Whalen, Mr. Elsworth
Whalen, Mrs. Josephine
Whittaker, Mr. Stephen
Wilks, Mr. Willie

Wilks, Mrs. Edna
Willoughby, Mrs. Johanna Ruth
Wilson, Doris
Wilson, Mattie
Wilson, Miss Lois (Brooklyn, NY)
Wilson, Miss Rosa (Brooklyn)
Wilson, Mrs. Lottie Belle

Watch Care Members

Epps, Mr. Arkey (Nazarene Baptist
Church, Blackstone, VA)
Epps, Mrs. Bertha
(Antiwar Baptist Church,
Crew, VA)
Mitchell, Mr. William
(Mount Zion Baptist Church,
Daytona Beach, FL)

Children

Johnson, Mary Louise (age 12)
McArthur, Master Joseph (age 10)
Roberts, Miss Betty Jane
Wilks, Master George R. (10)

This was the largest membership in church history, and it provided enough person power for twelve church boards to do their work: Trustee, Usher, Pastors Aide, Stewardess, Willing Workers, Missionary Society, Christian Endeavor, Senior Choir, Junior Choir, Deaconess, Benevolence, and Sunday School.

It also enabled the church to continue its fund-raising activities, decorate the basement, and renovate the altar. By August 1952 all bills had been paid, the pastor's monthly salary was raised from $36 to $39, a mimeograph machine was purchased, and the bank account ran a monthly balance of about $200. At the end of November Reverend Johnson entered exhibits in the Scout Hobby Show and won first Grand Prize,

---

𝕳arvest 𝕯inner

𝕾outhern 𝕱ried 𝕮hicken
THURSDAY, NOVEMBER 10, 1955
5 P. M. - 7 P. M.
In the Church Dining Hall

Sponsored by
Ladies of the Clinton A M E Zion Church

Donation $1.25   Rev. D. Woodson, *Pastor*

Ticket for the Harvest Dinner at the church in November 1955. Source: Clinton A. M. E. Zion Church archives.

---

a war bond series E, with a value of $25. He placed it in the basement fund to be used to beautify the church inside.

The church roll for 1954–1955 shows sixty-three members and fourteen out-of-town members. By 1955 the membership had declined to forty-one members. Part of the reported decline may have been due to a more stringent definition of membership, with only those who paid their general claims so counted. Part of the decrease was also caused by some members moving away. In 1958 ten moved away. The officers in that year were as follows:

W. A. Kelley .... Pastor
Wray M. Gunn .... Chairman
Sinclara Gunn .... Secretary
Mattie Bowen .... Treasurer
Joseph McArthur .... Steward
Pinkie Brooks .... Church clerk
Willie Wilks .... Trustee
Arkey Epps .... Trustee

134

Membership by 1963 had declined to twenty-seven members and then recovered in 1964, as reported by Mrs. Brooks in the Church Roll and Certificate Book: "36 on Active List although some of these don't attend regularly and pays no money only sometimes. 25 names on Inactive list. Never pays any church dues and give no support to Pastor and Church" (Clinton Church records). The boards for 1964–1965 were as follows:

Trustee Board
Mr. R. M. Gunn,
   Chairman
Mrs. Sinclara Gunn
Mrs. Pinkie Brooks
Mr. Joseph McArthur

Treasurer
Mrs. Edna Wilks

Stewards
Mr. Willie Wilks
Mr. E. Sanderson
Mr. Arky Epes
Mr. Donald Wilson
Mr. Steve Whittaker

Stewardess Board
Mrs. Mattie B. Wilson
Mrs. Gertrude Harris
Mrs. Sanderson
Mrs. Burnell Brooks
Mrs. Grace Zinnermon

Sunday School
Mrs. Edna Wilks
Loretta Bowens,
   assistant

Home Mission
Mrs. Mattie B. Wilson

Missionary Society
Mrs. Sinclara Gunn
Mrs. Pinkie Brooks

Pastors Aide
Mrs. Hattie Dixon
Mrs. Zinnermon
Mrs. Arlene Williams
Mrs. Salsbury
Mrs. Mary McArthur
Mrs. Mattie Bowen

Church Clerks
Mrs. Pinkie Brooks
Mrs. Edythe
   Sanderson

Willing Workers
Mrs. Clara Durante
Mrs. Gertrude George
Mrs. Alice McArthur
Mrs. Zelene Hamilton
Mrs. Juanita Woodson

Deaconess
Mrs. Mary McArthur
Mrs. Hattie Dixon
Mrs. Eirthie Rice

Class Leaders
#1 Mrs. Eirthie Rice
#2 Mrs. Florence Gunn
#3 Mrs. Eloise
   McArthur
Mr. Joseph McArthur,
   at large

Usher Board
Mrs. Lottie Belle
   Wilson
Mrs. Gertrude Harris,
   assistant

Assessment Fund
Mrs. Sinclara Gunn

Insurance
Mrs. Pinkie Brooks

Parsonage Committee
Mr. Joseph McArthur
Mr. Walter Zinnermon,
   assistant

By 1967 the membership had increased to fifty-one people and then declined to thirty-six adult members in 1968. In the middle years of the 1970s, there were about thirty-five to forty members, and in September 1978 the roll shows twenty-nine members:

Louise Brown

Angela Carthon

Alphonso Dozier (child)

Esther Dozier

Henry E. Dozier

Henry E. Dozier Jr. (child)

William Frady

C. Freeman

Clarence Gunn

David Gunn

Florence Gunn

Ray Gunn

Velma Gunn

Sinclara Gunn

Arthur Hemingway

Ida Hemingway

Jim Hollingworth

Jodie Hooks

Alice McArthur

Eloise S. McArthur

JoAnne Price

Peggy A. Rice

Martha Sharpton

Irene Taylor

Edna Wilks

Arlene Williams

Cyraneous Williams

Lottie B. Wilson

Mattie Wilson

Church Developments from 1950 to 1979

With a large and relatively stable membership, several dedicated members, a steadier flow of income, and a usable basement, the church was very active in the 1950s and 1960s. At times the books were balanced, and at other times there were bills not fully paid on time. Beyond member offerings, money was raised through suppers, teas, breakfasts, and bazaars and at the annual summer barbecue, usually held on the VFW grounds. Larger events were often held at St. James Episcopal Church.

The year of 1953 was a year of three firsts. A coal fund was established to deal with the cost of running the furnace, a major expense. Several members and groups pledged to support the new fund, with each (Mary Jones, Missionary Society, Pastors Aide, Stewardess Board, Willing Workers Club, Mrs. Simmons, Sunday school) buying a ton each, at $24.50 per ton. On 4 January the first church bulletin was distributed.

And near the end of the year, on 25 December, the church began the ritual of holding a sunrise service at six o'clock on Christmas morning.

The following year, on 24 June, Rev. David Woodson replaced Rev. Johnson as the pastor. Born in Brooklyn, Reverend Woodson was a graduate of Livingston College and a World War II veteran. He had previously led churches in Pennsylvania and Portland, Maine. Woodson was married to the former Mabel Harrison, and they had two children—Elizabeth and David Jr. In 1956 Reverend Woodson was named minister for migrant workers in the northern Berkshires by the Massachusetts Council of Churches. He had done similar work previously in Pennsylvania.

CLINTON A.M.E. ZION

CHURCH
Great Barrington Mass.

Date Issued _Sept. 17 1955_

To whom it may concern:

This is to say that _Josephine Whalen_ is a member of the above named church, and is hereby permited to collect funds in the name of Clinton A.M.E. Zion Church.

Permission granted by the chamber of Commerce of Great Barrington Mass. and the Trustees of the church.

Pastor _Rev. David Woodson Sr._

Chairman _Ellsworth Whalen_

A solicitation permit granted to Josephine Whalen in 1955. Source: Clinton A. M. E. Zion Church archives.

After Reverend Woodson became ill in 1957, in April Rev. N. Randolph Scott of New Haven assumed the Clinton pastorate; however, Reverend Scott was not in residence, coming up only to conduct Sunday services. Otherwise, the church was run by the membership. Reverend Woodson's illness and the visiting-pastor arrangement, which led to the irregular scheduling of Sunday services, evidently caused some disruption, and in the April 1957 Quarterly Report (Clinton Church records), the members commented: "The Church this quarter has not been very successful. We the Church as a body has slowed up in working and hope and trust our new year will be more successful in our work in God's kingdom. There have not been activities this quarter. The members are all upset over the way things has been going as far as the church has been concerned." This report seemed to invigorate the members, and fund-raising for the balance of the year was much more productive:

5/23	Dinner	128.40
6/16	Rally	100.10
6/27	Dinner	154.99
7/25	Summer Sale	94.75
8/1	Luncheon	26.00
8/8	Luncheon	13.31
8/9	Auction	71.50
8/22	Auction	34.87
9/5	Auction	31.79
9/19	Dinner	114.39
9/29	Mrs. Watkins	83.25
n.d.	Tree Rally	147.33
Oct.	Dinner	112.00
11/23	Thanksgiving Basket	205.75
11/24	Christmas Sale	27.00

Reverend Scott was succeeded in May 1958 by a new, full-time pastor, Rev. William Kelley, accompanied by his wife, Lillian, and two children. In 1959 the church converted to an oil furnace, and oil now replaced coal as a major expense. A furnace fund was started in 1960 to pay for the oil. During the 1960s the church came up with several new ways to raise

money. One was the Men versus Women Rally in 1962, with the men raising $79.60 and the women $243. A second was the State Rally, conducted
several times, in which members raised funds for "their" state. For example, in October 1963 the results were as follows:

Missouri $35.50
Kentucky 16.00
South Carolina 12.00
New York.................... 21.00
Alabama..................... 13.00
Connecticut 25.00
Mississippi.................... 5.35
Massachusetts............. 9.50

In 1957 the northern Berkshire Chapter of the Massachusetts Council of
United Church Women, under the leadership of Mrs. John Talbott of Wil-
liamstown, looked to expand into southern Berkshire County. The United
Church Women was a Christian ecumenical organization founded to sup-
port human rights, peace, and justice. One of the organization's major
activities was the annual World Day of Prayer observed each February or
March. On 8 March 1957 a World Day of Prayer service was held at the
United Methodist Church in Great Barrington, with Mrs. Sinclara Gunn

Great Barrington, Mass.
October 29, 1956

To Whom It May Concern:

The children of our churches, identified by the orange and black S O S armbands,
are collecting your donations for the Share Our Surplus Project. This will send
one pound of surplus food for each penny collected, to the needy of the world.
The money is not used to purchase the food, but rather to pay the postage from
this country to its destination. We feel sure you will wish to help in this
worthwhile project.

For the churches of the community,

Marjorie R. Evans.
Church School Superintendent
First Congregational Church

Fund-raising letter carried by children from town churches in 1956. Source: Clinton A.
M. E. Zion Church archives.

and Mrs. Pinkie Brooks on the organizing committee. On 2 May 1959 Fellowship Day was observed at the Clinton Church with a presentation by Mrs. Benson H. Harvey (of Southampton, Massachusetts), vice president of the United Church Women. And on 4 December 1959 the Berkshire Council of United Church Women met at the Clinton Church for installation of southern Berkshire officers, with Mrs. Pinkie Brooks as chairperson. Also involved from Great Barrington were Reverend Spyker and Mrs. Duval of the Congregational Church, Mrs. Orville De Rose of the United Methodist Church, Mrs. Martha Crawford and Mrs. Lloyd H. Height of the Macedonia Baptist Church, and Reverend Kelley and Mrs. Sinclara Gunn of the Clinton Church.

On 7 January 1960 a full slate of officers for the southern Berkshire Council was announced:

Mrs. Orville De Rose, Vice President
Mrs. Pinkie Brooks, Executive Chairman and Secretary
Mrs. Martha Crawford, Treasurer
Mrs. E. E. Duvall
Mrs. Lloyd Height
Mrs. Sinclara Gunn
Mrs. James O'Keefe
Mrs. John Francis—Egremont branch
Mrs. Maude Gorham

For the remainder of the decade, an ecumenical World Day of Prayer was held each year, rotating among different churches in town: St. James, United Methodist, St. Peter's, First Congregational, and Clinton in 1965 and 1966. In 1969 the women agreed to support a special project for the year on racial prejudice in the United States. Among Clinton women involved were Mrs. McArthur, Mrs. Wilks, and Mrs. Durante.

Reverend Kelley, in May 1962, was replaced by Rev. William Durante from Ansonia, Connecticut. Reverend Durante served for ten years until illness forced him to step down in 1972. He was one of the most influential leaders of the church and a community leader in town. His son, Willard H. Durante, assisted his father at the Clinton Church from 1970 to 1972 and later was pastor of the Price Memorial A. M. E. Zion Church in Pittsfield from 1976 to 2002. He also led the

Clinton A.M.E. Zion Church

April 22, 1956

Rev. David Woodson—Pastor

The Prelude

The Call to Worship

Processional Hymn————————————————————————————#231

Responsive Reading————————————————————————#6●●
#690 Peace

Hymn————————————————————————————————#402

Affirmation Of Faith

Hymn————————————————————————————————#276

Announcements——————————————————————Mrs. P. Brooks

Choir Selection

Prayer

Ministry Of Kindness

Hymn————————————————————————————#226

Lesson From The Holy Scripture

Choir Selection

Sermon

The Invitation To Christian Dicipleship

Offering

Recessional Hymn————————————————————————#26

****

Shut In
  Mrs. Rachel Freeman
  Miss. Etta Reynolds
  Mr. Edward Watkins

Announcements

1. General Claim Card
2. Church Dinner on April 26, 1956.. Mrs. Hattie Dixon-Chairman
3.

****

Let. Us...
      Live Together......
                And Love.....
                      One Another...............

This program is probably the first printed program used at the church for a regular Sunday service. Source: Clinton A. M. E. Zion Church archives.

Pittsfield branch of the NAACP from 1966 to 1982. The church record book for 27 May 1962 (Clinton Church records) notes Rev. William Durante's first meeting:

> *Rev. Durante New Pastor hold[s] first meeting. Open by singing Love Thine o Lord—Prayer by the Pastor Rev. Durante and few remarks of inspiration in behalf of his own life and ministery. Motion that everyone agree on that the Pastor move the things he wish[es] up her[e] for his convenience. Paint the Parsonage for Mrs. Durante the color she would like.*

In November Rev. Durante participated in the first Harvest Conference sponsored by the United Methodist Church, with additional representatives from the Congregational Church and Temple Ahavath Shalom. Participation with other local churches as well with other A. M. E. Zion churches in Massachusetts and Connecticut, which had started several decades earlier, continued in the 1960s with unity services and, in June 1966, with participation in an Interfaith Choral Group of twenty-six churches and four hundred "live voices" at Tanglewood. In this decade two new Black social groups emerged in Great Barrington—the Great Barrington Community Club and the Monday Nite Club. The latter sponsored a bus trip to the World's Fair in New York City in October 1965. And the Jolly #12 Club continued to meet as well. On 10 September 1967 this club held a barbecue at the home of Mrs. Zelene Hamilton at 118 Main Street. Often held thereafter at the VFW on south Main Street, the annual barbecue in August became a major social and fund-raising event for the church. The barbeque in 1974 raised $913.69.

Former pastor Rev. A. W. Johnson died in Michigan on 21 October 1970. His body was brought to the church for viewing before his funeral and burial in Ansonia, Connecticut.

In 1972 Reverend Durante became ill and had to step aside from the pastorate. His son, Willard Durant, of Pittsfield, briefly took over the pastorate, until Rev. James Little assumed it full time. On 21 October 1973 Reverend Little was absent, and Mrs. Fanny Cooper from Pittsfield conducted the service. Cooper was the founder of the Price Memorial A. M. E. Zion Church in Pittsfield in 1958. The church began in her living room on Columbus Avenue. Remaining active in the

DISTRICT CONFERENCE PROGRAM

HARTFORD DISTRICT OF THE NEW ENGLAND
CONFERENCE, CHURCH SCHOOL AND CHRISTIAN
ENDEAVOR, WOMEN'S HOME AND FOREIGN
MISSIONARY SOCIETY AND HOME MISSIONS
MASS MEETING
at

THE A. M. E. ZION CHURCH
DANBURY, CONN.

Rev. Leslie Lawson, Host Pastor

Thursday, Friday and Saturday
September 26, 27, 28, 1957

Rt. Rev. Wm. Jacob Walls, A.M., D.D., Presiding Bishop
Rev. Henry B. Norville, Presiding Elder
Rev. I. Atkins, Host Pastor

Each minister is asked to register one delegate from the Church School, Christian Endeavor, W.H.F.M. Society.

Registration—$10.00 per person for the three day period. All local Elders, Deacons, Exhorters, Superanuated and Missionary Evangelists are expected to register with $3.00.

MISSIONARY DISTRICT OFFICERS

Mrs. Dorothy Walls ....Episcopal District Supervisor
Mrs. Daisy E. Rudd ....General Chairman
           Life Members Council, A.M.E. Zion Church
Mrs. Cornelia Parks ....President of Women
Mrs. Sinclara Gunn ....Secretary of Young Women
Mrs. Ann Benford ....Supt. of Buds
Mrs. Inez Jefferson ....Pres. Life Members Council
Mrs. M. L. McDew ....Supply Captain
Mrs. Gladys Hunter ....Pres. Conference Workers

HOME MISSIONS

Mrs. Aurelia Jones ....President

CHRISTIAN EDUCATION OFFICERS

Mrs. De Vera Lockhart ....Episcopal District Director
Mrs. Grace Miller ....Assoc. Director of Conference
Mrs. Emma Davis ....Director of Adults
Miss Betty Swartz ....Director of Youth
Mrs. Anna Burress ....Director of Children
Mr. Clyde Smith ....District Director

Program for the District Conference in September 1957. Mrs. Sinclara Gunn is listed as Secretary of Young Women. Source: Clinton A. M. E. Zion Church archives.

THE BERKSHIRE COUNTY BRANCH
of the
National Association for Advancement of Colored
People

The
is one of
greatest c   Invites you to attend its Fifth Annual Dinner Dance, which will be
Ventfort Hai   held at The Festival House, Lenox, Mass.
one million c
stone, varicol
pannelling, inc   Saturday the Twelfth of September 1959
   On the groui
far corners of the   Semi-Formal
   The greats in
Holmes, Hawthorne, $5:00 per person
Morgans and Vanderbil
Berkshires. Now you m
unspoiled, with its lak
   The Festival House   Dinner 7 to 9
lawn, grounds and facilit   Dancing 8 until
town, You will find a cui
finest quality ingredients t   Cocktails will be served before dinner
   All for your exploration
welcome and hopes that you wil
with us before dinner on Septem.

Mrs Sinclara Gunn ..president
Mr Frank T. Walker... Chairman
Mr Lincoln A.Jones..Co-Chr
Information... Pittsfield Hi 31183

Reservation Deadline September 4,1959
Please Send Money with Reservations to 64
Orlando Ave. Pittsfield, Mass.

Number....   Amount $......
(Make all checks payable to Berkshire
County Branch N.A.A.C.P.)

North to
Vermont

West to
Albany

Pittsfield

Festival
House

Tanglewood

Lenox

Lee
Exit 2

Mass. Pike
To Boston

Exit #2

Stockbridge

South to N.Y.C. + Merritt Pkway

Flyer announcing the fifth annual dinner dance of the Berkshire County Branch of the NAACP in 1959. Source: Clinton A. M. E. Zion Church archives.

church, she eventually became a minister. In April 1975 she wrote to Black church pastors in the county saying she wanted to produce a video series on the county's Black churches for cable television viewing.

In August 1974 the Clinton membership was informed by Presiding Elder Rev. Warren E. Brown that the Clinton Church and the Price Memorial Church in Pittsfield were being transferred to the Boston District of the A. M. E. Zion Church. Reverend Brown also used the meeting to comment on what he perceived as a need for more careful administration and requested that additional insurance be purchased and church documents be secured. At the following quarterly meeting in November, Brown asked that account books be reviewed by the presiding elder at each Quarterly Conference. He also provided reporting forms to be filled in and signed by the chair of the trustee board. Reverend Brown's efforts to bring structural change evidently had an effect, and in February 1975 the membership voted eleven to three to ask the district conference not to return Reverend Little. In May Reverend Brown continued his efforts:

> The Elder also spoke on Crucifix[;] did not belong in AME Zion
> Church and did not want to see it there on Communion morning.
> A question was asked about the picture of the good shepherd
> be[ing] hung in the church. The answer was no picture should
> be hung in the edifice. Said a white cross could be hung inside.
> He said the church has the wrong [illegible]. Mrs. Eloise Mac
> Arthur took crucifix down as her husband donated it to go home
> with her. . . . P. E. said we need a Black man in town to walk the
> streets in Great Barrington. (Clinton Church records)

In 1975 Rev. Douglas E. Lawrence replaced Reverend Little and he oversaw the renovations. On 31 August the membership voted unanimously to designate Mrs. Pinkie Brooks "Mother of the Church" and began to plan a celebration in her honor. Unfortunately, Brooks died on 3 November, at seventy-seven years of age. She had come to Great Barrington from South Carolina in the early 1920s and joined the church in 1923. Her husband, Allen, died in 1934, and she devoted much of her time to the church and community activities. She served as clerk for many years, and this history has benefited from her careful records and accounts of meetings. She was a member of the Great Barrington Grange, the Republican Town Committee, the Southern Berkshire Republican Club, the Fairview Hospital Women's Auxiliary, and community singing societies in Great Barrington and Hudson, New York. As one of the first to own a car, Pinkie Brooks often drove other members to events outside the region. She also raised her niece, Eloise Mitchell (Page), who came to Great Barrington from Virginia.

From 24 to 28 November Rev. Earl Cheek of Albany, New York, conducted revival services at the church, and in May 1976 the Eugene Lawrence Brotherhood Chorus of Buffalo, New York, gave a concert and participated in Sunday evening services. In June 1976 Rev. John Cooper took over the pastorate from Reverend Lawrence, and Reverend Cooper remained in the position into the next decade. Cooper had formerly been pastor of the Price Memorial A. M. E. Zion Church in Pittsfield. The new pastor in Pittsfield was Rev. Willard Durant, former assistant pastor of the Clinton Church and son of former pastor William Durante. In December 1977 Reverend Cooper joined with other clergy in the southern Berkshires in signing a public statement objecting to retail businesses opening on Sunday in the weeks between Thanksgiving and Christmas.

During these decades the church lost several longtime and dedicated members:

1950 .... Fred Freeman (local preacher)
1955 .... Doris Wilson
1959 .... Edward Watkins
    (former chairman of the Trustee Board and deacon)
1960 .... Jennie Freeman
1962 .... Rev. Raleigh Dove (former pastor)
1965 .... Mary Jones
                    Josephine Whalen
1966 .... Joseph McArthur Sr.
1967 .... Washington Whittaker
1968 .... Stephen Whittaker
1969 .... Mary McArthur
1970 .... Rev. Alexander W. Johnson (former pastor)
                    James Salisbury
1971 .... Rebecca Smith

United Church Women of Massachusetts

DEPARTMENT OF MASSACHUSETTS COUNCIL OF CHURCHES

215 Melrose St,
Auburndale, Mass
Dec. 9, 959

Dear Mrs. Brooks,

Mrs. John Talbot Area Director for the Berkshires, of United Church Women, has written telling about the new Council; and giving me your name as President.

May I congratulate you on the forming of the Southern Berkshire Council, and send to you my very best wishes! If I can be of help with your World Day of Prayer plans I shall be happy to do so. If you are appointing a W.D.P. Chairman, would appreciate your sending me her name. If not, I'll mail any correspondence to you. Sincerely,

Ruth E. Bean (mrs. H.G.
World Day of Prayer Chairman for Massachusetts

A letter to Mrs. Pinkie Brooks congratulating her on her appointment as the president of the Southern Berkshire Council of the United Church Women of Massachusetts.
Source: Clinton A. M. E. Zion Church archives.

1974 .... William Sharpton
                          Hattie Dixon
                          Albert Brinson
                          Grace Zinnermon
                          Rev. William Durante (former pastor)
1975 .... Pinkie Brooks ("Mother of the Church")
1976 .... Joseph McArthur
1977 .... Burnell Brooks
1979 .... Cornelius Johnson

Civil Rights and Social Activism

During the 1950s and 1960s and into the 1970s, several members of the church along with other members of the Black community became active in civil and human rights and charitable activities. The Clinton Church itself took no official action, but the building was often used for meetings, fund-raising, and, no doubt, much private discussion that went unrecorded. The activities were meant to change the world—locally, regionally, nationally, and even internationally.

Much of the activity centered on civil rights and took place through the Pittsfield branch of the NAACP. Founded in 1919 (the NAACP was founded in 1909), the branch became inactive in the 1920s. It was revived in 1945 and remained the primary civil rights organization in the region into the 1980s. Although it was headquartered in Pittsfield, meetings were frequently held in South County as well.

One mysterious entry in the Clinton Church record books dates to early 1954. It comprises two pages of unedited notes from a meeting, although no information is provided on the exact time or location of the meeting. None of the attendees were Clinton members, save for Reverend Johnson, who was the guest speaker, and Mrs. Sinclara Gunn, who probably took the notes. The notes highlight some issues facing the local Black community at the beginning of the civil rights era.

Case of Mrs. Mildred Persip. Another Robert Nolan are being discriminated. [Nolan] has been shifted around at different jobs at General Electric. A Man should have 30 days to learn to operate on a job. He said he was in New York to meeting and the members

are working together. Its nice to believe that things are getting
better. Some jobs are taking some of the jobs to the far south and
the union are there to help to get the colored. White[s] are few.
Mr. Kennedy made motion seconded by Mr. Chambliss that
Mr. Shepard represent us at the General Electric.

The Berkshire County
NAACP. will meet
to day at 3. at St Johns
Hall, 173 Robbins
ave, Pittsfield. The
nominating committee
will be elected.
Please try to attend
this meeting. we
need a good attendance
to carry out the work.
Are you willing to
sacrifice for the
freedom of Others
who are depressed?,
S. Gum

An NAACP meeting announcement from the minute book of 1959. Source: Clinton
A. M. E. Zion Church archives.

Clean up hall for NAACP. Benefit to have social, have a
Barbecue P. Turn back to committee for further [discussion?].
Mr. Lafayette Walker, Assistant Secretary, suggestion
Chairman and Executive Board. Workshop Meeting in Regional
Conference. Mr. Shepard made motion that we send a delegate
to attend these meetings. Miss Pierce said she thought it was
treasurer reports showing account $100.00. Mrs. Sinclara
Gunn Delegate. Mr. Hart alternate Delegate. Rev. A. W.
Johnson introduced by Mr. [David] Gunn. Rev. Johnson subject
was 6 Chapter of [Isaiah] and few of our great men.

On 7 February 1954 the church made its first offering, $7.54, for the NAACP. Offerings were made several other times, although not every week for the NAACP. In May the offering was $6.45 and then $6.45 again in February 1955. On 13 February the Pittsfield branch of the NAACP held its regular meeting in South County at the Clinton Church, with Mrs. Pinkie Brooks in charge of refreshments. On 4 December the members made a special offering of $19.59 for the Montgomery, Alabama, boycott, and in March 1956, members of the church attended a prayer meeting at the Masonic Temple in Pittsfield in support of the boycott.

The Fight For Freedom has undertaken to raise the necessary funds.

We appeal to your to contribute what you can toward this fund and toward a united America, where citizens of all races can have equal opportunity for life, liberty and the pursuit of happiness.

Make checks payable to the Berkshire County Branch of the National Association For the Advancement of Colored People. Enclosed is an addressed envelope for your convenience.

Respectfully,

Myrtle M. Rollison, Chairman
Fight For Freedom Committee

Portion of an NAACP appeal letter distributed to church members in the early 1960s. Source: Clinton A. M. E. Zion Church archives.

As the decade moved on, race relations remained a major issue, and on 12 February 1959 over one hundred people attended a special service at the Great Barrington Congregational Church to observe Race Relations Sunday and Brotherhood Week. The event was organized by the Clinton, Macedonia Baptist, Congregational, St. James Episcopal, and United Methodist churches and was led by Rev. Fred Spyker of the Congregational Church, assisted by Reverend Kelley of the Clinton Church. It was of sufficient local impact to garner front-page coverage in the *Berkshire Courier*. On 11 October Mrs. Sinclara Gunn announced to the church that the NAACP would be meeting that afternoon in Pittsfield at three in the afternoon to elect officers. She urged people to attend, noting, "We need a good attendance to carry out the work." Mrs. Gunn and her husband, David Gunn Sr., were active in the NAACP and often traveled around the state and beyond on its behalf.

The 1960s saw civil rights continue to grow as a national issue. In June 1961 a Retreat Conference on Integration was held at Gould Farm in Monterey, Massachusetts, although it is not clear if there was any local involvement beyond Gould Farm members. The issue of racial discrimination in the Berkshires became more public in 1966 when *Courier* journalist John Mooney questioned the rationale for a decision by the

Clinton A. M. E. Zion Church

VISITORS CARD

Name *Mrs. Annette McCloe.*

Address *44 Eagle St.*

Bridgeport 7 Conn

Would you like to say something?
Check (X) Yes_____ No *No*____

We are glad to have you worship with us. Come again. You are welcome to all services. REV. W. A. Kelly, Pastor

Visitor Card used in the late 1950s and early 1960s. Source: Clinton A. M. E. Zion Church archives.

Sheffield selectmen to deny a club liquor license to Walter Lee Zinnermon, who was a member of the Clinton Church. In his column on 21 April Mooney editorialized that "we can't help wondering what the result would have been if Mr. Zinnermon hadn't been a Negro." He stayed with the issue in his next column on 28 April and also criticized another decision of Sheffield selectmen, to deny a permit to a summer camp to be run by the East Side Settlement House of New York City: "Nonetheless, lurking under the surface and never mentioned at the hearing—but pointedly mentioned in street-corner conversations in Sheffield later in the week—was the fact that the campers would have been largely Negro and Puerto Rican children from the city."

From 1967 through 1969 the local NAACP was especially active. The Clinton Church, as a religious institution, was not directly involved in these activities, although the church was used for meetings (as was the Macedonia Church) and members were active as individuals. Those in Great Barrington most involved were Mrs. Gunn (who lived in Stockbridge) and Mrs. Brooks, both of whom were active in the church as well, and Mrs. Elaine Gunn and Miss Mabel Gunn (until her death in

Announcement for the annual NAACP Dinner in 1968. Source: Clinton A. M. E. Zion Church archives.

Lime Kiln Road
Sheffield, Mass.
July 25, 1969

TO: Members of Clinton A.M.E. Zion Church

SUBJECT: CHURCH IMPROVEMENT CAMPAIGN

On, Friday, July 18, 1969, your Trustee Board signed an agreement with the 1st. Agricultural National Bank to borrow $1300.00 to finance a new roof for the church and parsonage. This agreement will be reimbursed to the bank at $43.50 per month over a period of 36 months with the first payment due on Sept. 1, 1969.

This is the first step in a larger improvement plan which the church officials are anticipating but since it is the most pressing problem, we secured the funds now. By the time we are finished with our improvements, we look forward to new siding and insulation plus an additional room in front. This overall project may require in the neighborhood of $10,000.00.

Your support is needed to help the church meet its obligations to the bank for the roof. We hope to raise this money for the roof through your pledges and contributions. For the rest of the project, we intend to set up, with the bank, a public solicitation program.

This informative letter is to ask each member and friend to fill out the pledge form at the bottom and return it to either Mrs. Pinkie Brooks or Mr. Ray Gunn before August 24, 1969. Questions will be answered by any of the Trustees.

Sincerely yours,

Ray M. Gunn

Ray M. Gunn, Chairman

I, *Pinkie Brooks* donate/pledge the sum of $ *200.00* per month, yearly or at one time to the Clinton A. M. E. Zion Church for the Church Improvement Fund. These contributions will be tax deductible.

Signed: *Pinkie Brooks*

The Church Improvement Campaign pledge letter sent to the members in July 1969. Source: Clinton A. M. E. Zion Church archives.

CERTIFICATE OF APPOINTMENT

of

LOCAL **HOME MISSION WORKER** PRESIDENT

in the

New England .... Annual Conference

CLINTON MEMORIAL, GREAT BARRINGTON

of the

African Methodist Episcopal Zion Church

THIS IS TO CERTIFY THAT Mrs. Pinkie Brooks

of the .... New England .... Annual Conference

of the African Methodist Episcopal Zion Church is hereby appointed as Home Mission Worker to solicit money to extend the borders of the Annual Conference.

Her commission ends .... June 4, ... 19 74

She is required to report her entire collection, $ 50.00 .... to the Annual Conference

which meets at Varick Memorial Church, New Haven

Done at Belmont Street A. M. E. Zion Church, Worcester, June 10, ... 19 73

.... , Bishop

Z 10

Home Mission Worker Certificate of Mrs. Pinkie Brooks. Source: Clinton A. M. E. Zion Church archives.

1959). Also involved was Ruth D. Jones (daughter of former pastor Rev. Raleigh Dove), who in 1965 terminated her membership in the Zion Church and joined the Congregational Church in Stockbridge. Active as well, in building the regional NAACP, was David Gunn Sr. of Stockbridge (Sinclara Gunn's husband). In April 1967 a national representative of the NAACP speaking at St. James Church refuted charges (being spread by the FBI) that some NAACP officials were Communists. On 11 June Bishop Stephen Gill Spottswood, bishop of the A. M. E. Zion Church and head the national NAACP, spoke to the Pittsfield NAACP and at the Price Memorial A. M. E. Zion Church in Pittsfield. And in October the local NAACP announced plans for discussion groups in area towns over the next two years.

In 1968 the Pittsfield branch of the NAACP became especially active in South County. In January, learning that Bishop Spottswood would preach at their church in March, the Clinton members quickly established a Bishop's Purse. On 21 January Bishop Spottswood preached at the A. M. E. Zion Church in Torrington, with Reverend Durante in attendance. The bishop did preach at the Clinton Church on 24 March, but there is no record of what he said. A dinner was held in the basement after the service. His visits invigorated the Pittsfield NAACP branch, and later in the year it announced plans for a local employment office in Great Barrington. In August what was meant to be a private discussion became a very public inquiry into alleged police brutality in Great Barrington. Initially the NAACP's involvement was a talk with police officials about alleged brutality directed at Black youths. The discussion was made public by the *Berkshire Eagle* and then the *Courier*. Officially the matter was never made public and seemed to disappear, although the *Courier* could not hold back from editorializing on 20 March 1969: "We can't help but wonder if perhaps the real problem is that whenever a black person is arrested 'police problems' are expected to happen. The NAACP becomes upset, the clergy carries on, and the general public is thrown into confusion."

The Fight For Freedom has undertaken to raise the necessary funds.

We appeal to your to contribute what you can toward this fund and toward a united America, where citizens of all races can have equal opportunity for life, liberty and the pursuit of happiness.

Make checks payable to the Berkshire County Branch of the National Association For the Advancement of Colored People. Enclosed is an addressed envelope for your convenience.

Respectfully,

Myrtle M. Rollison

Myrtle M. Rollison, Chairman
Fight For Freedom Committee

Fund-raising letter for the NAACP. Source: Clinton A. M. E. Zion Church archives.

155

Rev. Douglas E. Lawrence outside the church in 1976. Source: Clinton A. M. E. Zion Church archives.

That same week the Local Council of Churches formed a Human Relations Council with Rev. Lawrence A. Larson of St. James Episcopal Church and Wray Gunn (a trustee of the Clinton Church) as general chairmen. The council grew out of a series of discussions on race, youth, and housing issues in the region. Reverend Durante was chosen to lead the police relations subcommittee. In November Arthur L. Green, director of the Connecticut Commission on Human Rights and Opportunities, addressed the Human Relations Council at the Clinton Church.

One tangible outcome of the Council's work was the founding of Construct, Inc., in 1969. It was formed as a not-for-profit organization to secure state and federal finding to renovate existing property and build new affordable property in the town; the need for such an organization became clear during a session on "Housing and Poverty" held at the Clinton Church. In January 1970 the church paid $10 in dues to join Construct and has continued to support the organization ever since. In April 1973 the Clinton Church became Construct's temporary home when the organization began using the dining room as its office in return for half payment on the light bill and a donation toward the oil bill. Clinton trustee Wray Gunn was active in the organization from the beginning and served as treasurer and vice president and then president, beginning in 1975 and for the remainder of the decade. In Gerald Chapman's short history of Construct, Gunn's tenure is described: "His tenure has been highly successful, as many of the accomplishments previously detailed here were made under his jurisdiction. To preside at meetings of the Board and of sub-committees, he travels far—from Canaan[,] Connecticut or from Sheffield—and in presiding over such meetings, he conducts them expeditiously, moving them through the agenda with little loss of time." In 2006 Construct remains active in providing affordable housing.

Civil rights involvement continued into the 1970s. In October 1970 an NAACP meeting was held at the church, and on 5 June 1971 the Clinton Missionary Society opened the service at Price Memorial Church, with Reverend Spottswood the guest speaker. On 12 November 1972 Mr. Muse of the NAACP spoke at the Clinton Church's Quarterly Conference.

Despite its considerable involvement in civil rights, the church, as well as its members, did not seem to be much involved in the major civil rights controversy in town. This was the successful effort that began in 1967 and ended in 1969 with the establishment of a monument to W. E. B. Du Bois at his boyhood homesite on Route 23. The two most active community members were Mrs. Elaine Gunn and Mrs. Ruth D. Jones, neither a member of the church at the time, although Mrs. Gunn had been married in the church and Mrs. Jones was a member until 1965, when she left to join the First Congregational Church in Stockbridge. It was not until the twenty-first century, under the leadership of Pastor Esther Dozier, that the Clinton Church embraced Dr. Du Bois and actively promoted his legacy in town.

†

CHAPTER 7

Grandma's Church Promoting African American History

On 18 September 2005 the Clinton Church held its annual anniversary celebration. The sermon was offered by Rev. Nathaniel K. Perry of Belmont Street A. M. E. Zion Church in Worcester. His subject was reflected in the sermon's title, "What Happened to Grandma's Church." He commented that he found the topic especially relevant on that day because the Clinton Church was the closest he had seen in New England to "Grandma's Church." By *Grandma's Church* the pastor said he meant a church that was a refueling place, that believed prayer changed things, that had a desire to praise God and to live holy so as to experience the Holy Ghost. The size of the church made no difference—"a few people are the twigs that light the fire."

This adherence to tradition recognized by Reverend Perry continues to be one of the pillars of the Clinton Church. There are several others. A second is continuing support for and involvement in local social services and helping the poor and ill. A third, which emerged most strongly in the early twenty-first century, is its role as a repository and center for Black local history. A fourth, related to the third one, is the church's role in increasing public acknowledgement of W. E. B. Du Bois in Great Barrington and promoting his legacy in town. And, last, the church has maintained its long tradition of organizing and participating in interfaith services and programs.

All of this has persisted during a period of declining membership. The number of members has decreased because of the smaller Black population in Great Barrington, an aging Black population, declining church attendance in general, and the presence of two Black churches in town. But, while the membership has shrunk into the teens and attendance on Sunday is usually small, the church in the twenty-first century has become a very visible force in Great Barrington life. Under the leadership of its first female pastor, Rev. Esther Dozier, it has continued to participate in interfaith and civic activities, has promoted the legacy of W. E. B. Du Bois, and has been actively involved in studying and documenting African American history in the Berkshires.

The 1980s

The 1980s opened with an ugly incident of racism in town. In late 1979 a Black couple, Kenneth and Irene Taylor, rented a house on Giddings Street, off Route 23, east of where they had lived with their great-granddaughter Dawn. Shortly after moving in, their lives were disrupted by threatening phone calls, a stink bomb thrown through their window, and the garage door set on fire. The investigation by the local police proceeded slowly, and in February 1980 Henry Dozier Sr., a member of the Clinton Church, went before the Board of Selectmen and complained about the harassment and slow police response. By the end of the month, the local police, state police, and the FBI were at all at work looking for the perpetrator. They arrested Karen Gauthier, a local white woman living in Housatonic, Massachusetts, who openly objected to Black people living in the formerly all-white neighborhood. She was tried and convicted in Springfield and sent to federal prison for six months. The community was shocked by the incident, and to encourage racial and ethnic harmony, an ethnic fair was held in September at the St. Peter's Church hall on Cottage and East streets. Usually represented were the Black, Polish, German, Jewish, Irish, Italian, Greek, Lebanese, Alsatian, and American Indian communities with Clinton women serving at the Black food booth. The festival became an annual event, continuing into the 1990s.

In July 1982 Rev. James M. Hubert was appointed the new pastor. He had formerly led the Gardner Memorial A. M. E. Zion Church in

Reverends John Parron, Willard Durant, Fanny Cooper, and James Henderson in August, 1990. Source: Clinton A. M. E. Zion Church archives.

Springfield for seventeen years and before that the Cavalier A. M. E. Zion Church in Detroit for fifteen years. He also managed the Camp Barber church retreat in West Granville, Massachusetts, for thirteen years. Accompanying him was his wife, Dorothy, and the couple had three grown children—Arthur L., Kevin D., and Jacqueline.

On 11 December at a testimonial dinner at the Masonic Hall, Clinton members gathered to honor Edna Wilks for her service to the church. Wilks had been a member for forty-two years. Evelyn West and Fadie Hooks co-chaired the event, Betty Lou Carthon was mistress of ceremonies, and Esther Dozier served as the speaker. The day 12 December was designated as Edna Wilks Day at the church. Wilks held many positions at the church: pianist and music director, superintendent of the Sunday school, president of the missionary society, and, finally, chair of the board of trustees. She continued to serve until her death in 1997.

In 1982 the church celebrated its one hundredth anniversary. Reverend Hubert issued the following statement to mark the occasion:

What does the Centennial of a church say to us? Our Lord, in Matthew chapter seven suggests to us, the church like other organizations, is affected by the vicissitudes of the past century.

What have been some of the trials of the previous one-hundred years? Clinton had some misfortunes because of some of its leadership. She has endured some undermining influences. Our church has, of a certainty, been affected by some external negative forces. Of course, the church could not exist for one-hundred years without suffering violence from her enemies in some form. However, Jesus forewarned us of this. But Clinton, unlike many other organizations and businesses that began in 1882, still stands, rendering service to the community. What is the reason for this? The Lord gives us the answer. Clinton has stood for ONE-HUNDRED YEARS, BECAUSE, "IT WAS FOUNDED UPON THE ROCK." So, in spite of change and diversity, let us pray for strength renewed to carry on in the next century.

To all who have been and are now on the scene, we dedicate this Journal to their memory and to the glory of God.

May God richly bless and guide you as we commence the next one-hundred years.

James M. Hubert. Minister

Black history was first recognized publicly in the United States in 1926 with the celebration of the second week of February as Negro History Week. The celebration was initiated by African American scholar Carter G. Woodson, who chose this particular week because it was the week in which both Frederick Douglass and Abraham Lincoln were born. The calendrical recognition later became Black History Month. In 1983, a few weeks late, on 13 March, the Clinton Church first celebrated Black History Month, with guest speaker Sally Singleton from the Gardner A. M. E. Zion Church.

In 1984 Reverend Hubert was elected to the board of directors of the Southern Berkshire Community Action, which later became the Community Development Corporation. On 25 August he conducted the marriage of Valerie Wilson of Great Barrington and Darryl Logan of South Carolina at the church. The year marked the two-hundredth anniversary of Methodism in America, and on 18 November the church shared joint services with the United Methodist Church. Reverend Hubert and Rev. C. Elsie Dame of the United Methodist Church officiated, and the choirs from both churches provided musical selections.

The year of 1985 began with the news of the death, in Boston on 19 January, of Minnie Wheeler Dove, age 93, the widow of former pastor Rev. Raleigh Dove. On 28 July Dorothy Belle (Taylor) Hubert, wife of Reverend Hubert, died at Fairview Hospital at age sixty-six. The funeral was held on 3 August at the First Congregational Church. In October Bishop George W. Bashore, spiritual leader of the United Methodist Church of New England, visited Great Barrington and Reverend Hubert participated in joint service with Reverend Dame of the local Methodist church.

Marking the following year (1986) were several major events. Black History Month was celebrated with a week of events highlighted by a talk by Carol Burnett of Alford, Massachusetts, entitled "A Black

The Clinton Church's sister church, the Mt. Carmel A. M. E. Zion Church, in Nigeria in the 1990s. Source: Clinton A. M. E. Zion Church archives.

Edna Wilks at the Kwanzaa celebration in January 1997. Source: Clinton A. M. E. Zion Church archives.

American Visits Africa." On 28 February Reverend Hubert lost his son, Arthur Louis Hubert, who died at age forty. The funeral service was conducted by assistant pastor Samuel V. Henderson. Other clergy participating were Fanny Cooper (Warren Brown A. M. E. Zion Chapel in North Adams), C. Elsie Dame (United Methodist Church), John Parron (Good Samaritan A. M. E. Zion Church in Pittsfield), Willard Durant (Christian Center in Pittsfield), N. Roosevelt Scott of New Haven, and Joseph Forte (Macedonia Baptist Church).

On 1 March of that year, the trustees launched a fund-raising drive under the chairperson Edna Wilks. The campaign was scheduled to run through October with the proceeds to be used to renovate the basement. Reverend Hubert was quoted in the *Berkshire Courier* (6 March 1986, 3): "Clinton was organized in 1882. This makes it a historical organization, having given continuous service to the community for 104 years."

October was a big month for Reverend Hubert. On the fourth he re-married, to S. Corrine Dean of Detroit. She had that year retired from teaching in the Detroit school system. Then, on the twelfth, he was honored at a party for his forty-three years in the ministry and thirty-seven as a pastor. Assistant pastor Henderson chaired the event, and the guest speaker was Rev. Warren Matthew Brown, presiding elder of the Boston district of the New England Conference.

The Clinton Church held a public Thanksgiving dinner on 27 November, attended by seventy-five people, at the United Methodist Church hall. Church members who cooked and served were Dean Pringle, Willie Wilks, Edna Wilks, Reverend Hubert, Alice McArthur, Clara Bell Zinnermon, Betty Lou Carthon, Eloise McArthur, and Donald Wilson.

Black History Month in 1987 was highlighted with a talk on Black history before 1620 by Elaine Gunn, longtime Great Barrington resident and teacher at Bryant Elementary School. On 24 February Rosa White died in Fairview, Massachusetts, at age 102, and her sister Etta Reynolds died a week later on 2 March at age 93. They were the daughters of Frank and Etta Frasier Reynolds. Born in South Carolina, they moved to Great Barrington early in the twentieth century with their parents. Both worked as housekeepers and nannies and were active in the church, White having been the organist for many years. On 14 July Susie Brinson died at age 88 in Meriden, Connecticut, at the home of her daughter Eloise B. Woods. She and her husband, Albert Brinson, were pioneer Black entrepreneurs, opening Brinson's Cleaners on Main Street in the 1920s and operating it into the 1970s. Her funeral was held on 18 July at the church.

Also that month, the church moved in a new interfaith direction when on the nineteenth it hosted members of Congregation Ahavath Sholom (CAS). Reverend Hubert shared the pulpit with CAS spiritual leader Sheldon Rothberg. (CAS was the first synagogue in Great Barrington and was founded in the 1920s.) The initiative continued in January 1988, when, on the fifteenth and seventeenth, the church and CAS shared services in each other's sanctuaries to mark Martin Luther King Jr.'s birthday. January also saw a chicken and spaghetti dinner catered by Willie Wilks.

Black History Month in February 1988 concluded with an address by Rev. Alexander Jamison Sr. of the Second Congregational Church in Pittsfield. Providing music were the Second Congregational, Price Memorial, and Macedonia Baptist church choirs. On 28 February, before transferring to the Hood Memorial A. M. E. Zion Church in Providence on 6 March, Reverend Hubert delivered his final sermon, "The Future Unveiled," at the Clinton Church. The service drew several other clergy, including Rev. Joseph Forte and the Macedonia Baptist congregation and Rev. John Parron and the Good Samaritan A. M. E. Zion Church congregation. Also present were Rev. and Mrs. Harry Almong, representing the special ministry of moral rearmament of the Reformed Church of America. Tributes to Hubert were offered by Rev. Fanny Cooper of Warren Brown A. M. E. Zion Church in North Adams, Rev. John Parron, Reverend Durant of Price Memorial, and Deacon Charles Moody of Macedonia Baptist Church. On 11 June the church joined with eleven others from South Berkshire County to present interfaith sacred music at Simon's Rock College. Reverend Hubert was replaced by assistant pastor

The 114th anniversary celebration in 1998. Seated from left to right are Henry Dozier, Esther Dozier, Rev. John Parron, Caroline Parron, Barbara Ross, and Retha Hollingsworth. Source: Clinton A. M. E. Zion Church archives.

Samuel Henderson for a brief period and then by Reverend John Parron from Pittsfield in 1989.

Parron served until 1999, when he moved to Mesa, Arizona, with his wife, Caroline. Reverend Parron had left the Lutheran Church to join the Price Memorial A. M. E. Zion Church in Pittsfield, where he trained as a local preacher. He then founded the Good Samaritan A. M. E. Zion Church, a mission church, in his home on John Street. He was appointed pastor of the Clinton Church in 1989 when supply pastor Samuel Henderson transferred to Amherst, Massachusetts. Reverend Parron was the church's first and only white pastor.

The 1990s

By the 1990s the church membership had shrunk to fewer than twenty, and fewer still regularly attended. The church rolls for 1992 to 1995 show the following members:

Rev. John R. Parron	Peggy Sands
Caroline Parron	Pauline Harris
Henry Dozier Sr.	Mattie Wilson
Esther Dozier	Clara Zinnermon
Pauline Harris	Edna Wilks
Fadie Boone	Evelyn West
Eloise McArthur	Wray M. Gunn Sr.
Retha Hollingsworth	Barbara Ross
Betty Lou Carthon	Edward Williams

During this period the church also added some new members, but their numbers did not replace the losses due to people moving away or passing away. The church rolls show the following new members (most probationary) for 1994–1998: Kathryn Dobson, Leah Reed, Roberta Balawn, Virginia Conway, Earl Neill, Jordan Loder, Theresa Watford, and Kelly Dozier.

Those from the church community who passed away in the 1980s and 1990s were the following:

1985 .... Dorothy Belle Hubert (wife of the pastor)
1986 .... Florence Gunn
                               Arthur L. Hubert (son of the pastor)
                               Martha Sharpton
                               Irene W. Wilks
1987 .... Rosa White
                               Etta Reynolds
                               Susie Brinson
1989 .... Ralph Darius Petty
1990 .... Alice McArthur
                               Eloise Page
1991 .... Sinclara Gunn
                               James Hollingsworth
1992 .... Walter Zinnermon
                               David McArthur Jr.
1993 .... Willie Wilks
                               Dolores Oakley Gunn
1994 .... Alice Williams
1995 .... Clara Durante
                               (wife of former pastor William Durante)
1997 .... Edna Wilks

In April the church held a revival for the first time in some years. It was led by Rev. John Anderson of the Goodwin A. M. E. Zion Church in Amherst. Choirs from Clinton and the Second Congregational Church in Pittsfield provided the music.

On 1 September 1991 Mrs. Sinclara Gunn died at age eighty-eight. She had been a member of the church for over forty-five years and held several church offices as well as having been active in the New England Conference. Born in Benson, Alabama, she graduated from Hampton Institute in Virginia, taught school in Alabama, and was a social worker in South Carolina. In 1926 she married David Gunn, and they moved to Lee in 1942 and then to Stockbridge in 1945. They were active in the NAACP, and she served as president and treasurer of the regional chapter. She was also a member of the Order of the Eastern Star, Grange, and the Council on Aging. Her funeral at the First Congregational Church in Stockbridge was conducted by Rev. David M. Lockhart and Clinton pastor John Parron.

Rev. Dozier, members, and visitors in front of the church in 2002.
Source: Karen Christensen.

The Clinton Church became involved publicly for the first time in honoring W. E. B. Du Bois in 1994. On 15 May the Clinton and the Macedonia church choirs sang hymns and spirituals for the dedication of historical markers at the Du Bois birth site (51 Church Street) and at the Mahaiwe Cemetery marking the graves of Du Bois's wife Nina and son Burghardt. Reverend Parron spoke at the cemetery dedication. Later that month Edna Wilks was elected to a three-year term on the board of the Great Barrington Historical Society.

The church officers for 1995 were as follows: president, Edna Wilks; treasurer, Peggy Sands; and secretary, Caroline Parron. In January Reverend Parron participated with clergy from other town churches at the Martin Luther King Jr. birthday celebration at the Macedonia Baptist Church. Later in the year there were continuing efforts to help the less fortunate. A community dinner in October raised money for the homeless, and food and money were also collected for Construct, the social service agency. A note in the Missionary Society minute book for 10 December recorded that "Madam president spoke of helping the needy in our community." Her call for help was heard, and in January 1996 money was collected and donated for World Hunger Day. In August 1996 the members decided to make fruit baskets to give the area poor for Thanksgiving and Christmas, and in November food was donated to the town food bank. In December the church celebrated Kwanzaa for the first time.

Efforts to help the poor were kept up in 1997. In January and April there were again collections for the World Day of Hunger. In June Esther Dozier suggested a project in which members would adopt a resident of a local nursing home; the project became reality in September. And in October $25 was given to Construct for its walk for the homeless.

Church president Edna Wilks died in 1997 and was replaced in February 1998 by Virginia Conway. The good works continued, and the winter calendar of events had now expanded to include Kwanzaa, Martin Luther King Jr. Day, and Black History Month, along with Christmas. In November 1998 the minutes record that the members "discussed how we could do an outreach in community for Christmas, Red Cross & YMCA. [Have] asked for donations of goodies for troop. We are going to participate in that. Sis Dozier is going to contact nursing homes to see about patients who don't have family or friends to celebrate the season and maybe give us names and sizes to donate something warm to them for Christmas. Also going to [do] our collection of food for the Food Pantry."

During the 1990s the church also helped build the Mt. Carmel A. M. E. Zion Church in Nigeria, with which Clinton established a sister-church relationship. The pastors of the new church were Rev. Cheta Izogo and Rev. Princewill Ewoh.

Reverend Esther Dozier and the Celebration of Black History and W. E. B. Du Bois

Esther Ballard Dozier was born and grew up in rural Alabama. She came to Great Barrington with her sister Mattie to join their sister Pearlie and brother-in-law Elijah Conway. In 1965 she married Henry Dozier, also from Alabama, at the Clinton Church. Although a Baptist, she joined the church in 1966, since Henry was a Methodist. Henry spent most of his career at Pfizer/Mineral Technologies in Canaan, Connecticut, and Reverend Dozier worked for thirty-five years at the Becton-Dickinson plant, also in Canaan. She was active in the church and held the position of exhorter when in 1999 the presiding elder, Nathaniel Perry, asked her

W.E.B. Du Bois
135th Birthday Celebration

Saturday, February 22, 2003
2:00 P.M.
Clinton African Methodist Episcopal Zion Church
Great Barrington

WELCOME

Rev. Esther Dozier
Pastor, Clinton African Methodist Episcopal Zion Church

MUSICAL SELECTIONS

Clinton African Methodist Episcopal Zion Church

KEYNOTE SPEAKER

Dr. Homer (Skip) Meade
Senior Area Director, National Evaluation Systems, Inc.

MUSICAL SELECTIONS

Price Memorial African Methodist Episcopal Zion Church

COMMENTARY

Randall O. Westbrook
Educator, social commentator, historian, and faculty member at
Fairleigh Dickinson University, Madison New Jersey

MUSICAL SELECTIONS

Macedonia Baptist Church

OPEN DISCUSSION

Program for the 2003 W. E. B. Du Bois 135th Birthday Celebration on 22 February 2003. Source: Clinton A. M. E. Zion Church archives.

to consider becoming the church's pastor. Later that year she was appointed the church's first female pastor, and in 2000 she was ordained by Bishop George W. Walker.

Under Reverend Dozier's leadership the church has been at the forefront in promoting local Black history and especially the legacy of W. E. B. Du Bois. The first major public event took place on 9 June 2001 and centered on the program "Honoring Our History: A Celebration of W. E. B. Du Bois," held at the St. Peter's Roman Catholic hall on Cottage Street. The event featured reflections and music by the Jubilee School of Philadelphia students and faculty; remarks by Du Bois's stepson, University of Massachusetts professor David Graham Du Bois; and musical selections by the Clinton Church and Macedonia Baptist Church choirs. Concluding the event was everyone singing "Lift Every Voice and Sing," the African American national anthem, written in 1900 by part-time Great Barrington resident James Weldon Johnson.

In September 2002 the W. E. B. Du Bois River Garden was dedicated, with Reverend Dozier delivering a welcome and the church choir along with the Price Memorial A. M. E. Zion Church choir from Pittsfield providing musical selections. The River Garden was conceived by Rachel Fletcher of Great Barrington as a memorial to Du Bois and to his interest in the local environment and the Housatonic River. Ms. Fletcher also worked with Reverend Dozier on the church's programs honoring Du Bois and Black history.

On 22 February 2003 the church launched a $20,000 fund drive with a program celebrating the 135th birthday of Du Bois at the church. The choirs of the Clinton and Price Memorial churches provided musical selections. Dr. Homer ("Skip") Meade of National Evaluation Systems, Inc., was the keynote speaker. Meade had formerly been a social studies teacher at Monument Mountain Regional High School, where he introduced a Black studies course in the 1970s. Additional commentary was offered by Professor Randall O. Westbrook of Fairleigh Dickinson University in Madison, New Jersey.

In the summer of 2003 the Department of Anthropology at the University of Massachusetts at Amherst conducted its third Summer Archaeological Field School at the W. E. B. Du Bois Boyhood Homesite on Route 23. Professor Robert Paynter ran the field school. A laboratory and interpretative center was set up at the Clinton Church where artifacts collected

Wray Gunn, former trustee Board chairman in February, 2006. Source: Karen Christensen.

at the site were processed, with some displayed to the public on tables on the front lawn. As part of the field school, lectures by Professor Warren Perry of Central Connecticut State University and Professor David Graham Du Bois were given on 1 and 6 August, respectively, with the Clinton Church acting as host.

The church commemorated its 121st anniversary on the weekend of 20–21 September 2003. On Saturday church historian David Levinson reviewed highlights and key people in the church's history, and local historian Bernard Drew furnished additional commentary. Sunday, as

Reverend Dozier pointed out, was the day for religion, with Rev. Alfred Johnson, pastor of the Gardner Memorial A. M. E. Zion Church of Springfield providing the sermon, and his church choir the musical selections. Dinner followed in the church dining hall.

Commemorations continued on 21 February 2004 with the marking of Du Bois's 136th birthday. The event was held at St. Peter's community hall, with Professor Westbrook the speaker and music provided by the choirs of the Clinton Church, Macedonia Church, Price Memorial Church, and Second Congregational Church of Pittsfield. On 18 and 19 September the church marked its 122nd anniversary with a sermon by Reverend Dozier on Saturday and a performance by the Price Memorial choir. On Sunday Rev. Clyde Talley of the Goodwin Memorial A. M. E. Zion Church in Amherst delivered the sermon, and his choir the music.

On 17 February 2005 the church celebrated Du Bois's 137th birthday. The guest speaker was Professor MaryNell Morgan, of Empire College, who discussed Du Bois's use of the sorrow songs in his *The Souls of Black Folk* and who led the assembled in singing. It was a day of mixed emotions, since the event was dedicated as well to the remembrance of David

Evelyn and Moses Haile, who were members in the 1940s and longtime neighborhood residents, in February 2006. Source: Karen Christensen.

Graham Du Bois, Du Bois's stepson and founder of the W. E. B. Du Bois Foundation, Inc., who had passed away recently. Leading a tribute to him was his colleague at the University of Massachusetts, Professor Paynter. The 17 and 18 September church anniversary celebration later that year featured the Price Memorial Choir on Saturday and a sermon by Rev. Nathaniel K. Perry of the Belmont Street A. M. E. Zion Church in Worcester and musical selections by his youth choir. Also present, on 18 September, was Mary Bridgemahon, the daughter of former pastor Rev. Alexander W. Johnson, who served in the church from 1951 to 1954. She recalled her years as a young girl in town living in the parsonage, memories of which included the fine dinners prepared for the community, children being taught how to behave, and how she felt very comfortable living in Great Barrington.

In 2005 the church hosted two events, and Reverend Dozier participated in a third, related to the African American Heritage Trail project led by Rachel Fletcher and Professor Frances Jones-Sneed of Massachusetts College of Liberal Arts. In May a panel discussing W. E. B. Du Bois received a large audience at the South County Community Center. Reverend

Rev. Dozier and her husband Henry in February 2006. Source: Karen Christensen.

Dozier was the only African American panelist, and she spoke emotionally and eloquently about what it meant to be a Black person in contemporary America, making the point that the color line Du Bois wrote about had not yet vanished. In June local historian Bernard Drew spoke at the church about the origins of the Black community in the southern Berkshires, based on his recent archival research in Sheffield. On 12 September the church hosted a panel on African Americans in South Berkshire County. Two of the panelists were former Clinton Trustee Board chairman Wray Gunn and his cousin by marriage, Elaine Gunn, who had been married in the church. They discussed their experiences growing up and living in South Berkshire County.

In 2006 the church joined with four other organizations to sponsor the Friends of the Du Bois Homesite. The organization was formed to work with the University of Massachusetts, which is trustee of the site for the state, to preserve the site and make it accessible to the public.

Some people involved in the *African American Heritage in the Upper Housatonic Valley* book, in the church in 2006. Left to right: Frances Jones-Sneed, Rachel Fletcher, Robert Paynter, David Levinson, and Bernard Drew. Source: Karen Christensen.

Children of the church at the annual Du Bois celebration in February 2006. Source: Karen Christensen.

On 25 February the church held its fourth annual Du Bois birthday celebration, with a standing-room-only crowd. Reverend Dozier commented that she wished she could have but half the number present at her Sunday service. The guest speaker was Professor William Strickland of the W. E. B. Du Bois Afro-American Studies Department at the University of Massachusetts at Amherst. Jay Schafer, the head of the libraries at the university, also spoke, sharing both the university's efforts to recognize Du Bois and the university's future plans. The event was dedicated to the recently departed Eloise Brinson of Meriden, Connecticut, and Ruth D. Jones of Boulder, Colorado, both former Great Barrington residents and members of the church. Music was provided by the children of the church and the Macedonia Baptist Church. On 19 March the Unitarian Universalist Church on Main Street held a peace vigil, attended by 200 people, on the third anniversary of the war in Iraq. Reverend Dozier was one of the speakers and offered a prayer for peace: "Lord, we pray for your Blessing and strength . . . as we try to cope with this deadly war. Lord, let there be peace on Earth, and let it begin with us."

In September 2006 the African American Heritage Trail through the Berkshires and northwest Connecticut was launched. The project was a regional effort that involved dozens of people and organizations. The church and Rev. Dozier were actively involved in planning the trail and compiling *African American Heritage in the Upper Housatomic Valley,* a book-length history of the African American life in the region and a guide to the trail. The trail and the book were of enormous significance to the African American community as they lifted the veil of invisibility that hid for many generations their presence and contributions in the Berkshires.

On 14 September the trail was officially opened with a ceremony at the Col. Ashley House in Sheffield. Rev. Dozier closed the event with the following prayer, which also seems a very fitting end for this account of the church's first 136 years:

God of our weary years.
God of our secret tears.
Who has brought us this far on our way. If it had not been for
*   you on our side, where would we be?*
We thank you O God for the means by which you used in the
*   person of Elizabeth Freeman, affectionately known as*
*   "Mum Bett," to change the course of history.*
We are thankful for everyone who was instrumental in making
*   this day possible.*
I know that you are smiling down on us and saying,
*   "At last they finally got it right."*

Amen

CHAPTER 8

A Death, Decline, and Salvation

A
bout eight o'clock in the morning of 11 June 2007, I had just settled at my desk in my office above Great Barrington's Mahaiwe Theater on Railroad Street when the phone rang. On the other end was a reporter from the Albany NPR station with some questions about Esther Dozier. She said she couldn't tell me why she was calling but she seemed legitimate and rushed, so I answered her questions as best I could. Troubled by the call, I immediately called my and Esther Dozier's friend Rachel Fletcher. She was very upset and told me that she had just gotten the terrible news that Esther had died. Even worse, rumor had it that she had been stabbed to death in her bed that morning and that Henry, her husband of forty-two years, was suspected of the crime and that police were searching for him. This news was an incredible shock not just to me but also, as it spread, to the entire community. And the shock only deepened when later in the morning Henry was arrested in his car in Lenox and that by all indications he was the perpetrator.

The story unfolded over the next few days. Henry had crashed his truck in town early that morning and was found a bit later by Great Barrington police wandering around a shopping center. The police picked him up and drove him home, dropping him off at about six o'clock. Later he called his son Alphonso and asked him to come to the house. As Alphonso arrived, Henry left, passing him in the hallway and then driving off in the family car. Alphonso discovered his slain mother and called the police, who came to the house, secured the scene, and went looking for Henry. His car was spotted in Lenox and he was taken into custody without resistance. Claiming he had drunk poison, he was taken to Berkshire Medical Center, examined and cleared, and then incarcerated in the county jail in Pittsfield.

Henry was charged with Esther's murder and placed in the Bridgewater State Hospital, a facility for the criminally insane. There was much discussion, rumor, and worry in the Great Barrington community over the next months about why Henry had done it and what would happen to him. It was all very mysterious and unnerving. Henry was not known to be a violent man, and by all accounts the Dozier's had had a happy marriage. Henry had been a deacon in the Clinton Church and was well known and liked around town. There was also considerable concern about the well-being of Esther and Henry's children and their families, especially since Esther had been the emotional and spiritual force that held the family together. There was concern as well about the Clinton Church, as again, Esther had been the force which kept the church going. Finally, in June 2009, Henry's case moved toward resolution. He appeared before Berkshire Superior Court Judge John A. Agostini in a jury-waived trial, and was found not guilty by reason of insanity on single counts of second-degree murder, leaving the scene of a property-damage accident, and operating to endanger. He was then returned to Bridgewater State.

The Funeral

After Esther's death, the first order of family, church, and community business was her funeral. Yet the circumstances and shock of her death, and the various worlds she lived in—the church, interfaith cooperation, social activism, African American heritage—led to some confusion and cross-purposes. The Northeastern Episcopal District of the A. M. E. Zion Church quickly took control, with Presiding Elder Margaret R. E. Lawson serving as its representative. Surveying the situation in Great Barrington, she was surprised to discover that Esther had been involved in so many activities. The district officials knew nothing of these activities as in her reports, Esther stuck to church affairs and never mentioned her other activities nor her reputation in the Berkshires as an effective activist for social justice and African American heritage. Esther's obituary spoke to these activities:

Rev. Dozier's community activities and influence went far beyond the church and the African American community. She spoke passionately against injustice, intolerance and most recently the war in Iraq. She believed that the church was a refueling place and that prayer could change things through a desire to praise God and live a holy life. (The Berkshire Eagle, 15 June 2007).

With her newfound appreciation of Esther's activities and influence, Rev. Lawson worked with Esther's friend and sister activist Rachel Fletcher, to expand the funeral service to include a few participants of the many who wanted to speak and who would offer remarks paying homage to these many dimensions of Esther's life and her contributions to the community.

Another issue facing Rev. Lawson was the wish of some Clinton members to have the funeral at the Clinton Church. If Esther had been just a member of the church, the Clinton Church would be the appropriate venue. But, as hundreds of people were expected and the Clinton Church could squeeze in only about eighty, it was not logistically possible. Instead the funeral was to be held in the large First Congregational Church (which W. E. B. Du Bois and his mother had attended) which could handle a crowd that size. A compromise was reached with the Clinton's members and a private ceremony was held at Clinton the day before the public service at the Congregational Church.

With the conflicts resolved and representatives from several dimensions of Esther's life included, the funeral was held at eleven o'clock in the morning of 18 June 2007. The sanctuary was full, with perhaps as many as four hundred people attending. So many came to the funeral that for the first time in anyone's memory traffic on Main Street came to a standstill. The right side of the sanctuary was filled with rows of several dozen A. M. E. Zion clergy and seated behind them several more rows of other clergy representing every Christian denomination and synagogue in the region. The center pews were filled by those who considered themselves Esther's family.

Over a dozen individuals offered prayers or remarks. Great Barrington Selectman Peter Fish and State Senator Ben Downing represented the local and regional governments. Senator Downing's remarks, whose respect for Rev. Dozier and her work was already well known, was especially moving and personal:

There are pictures which speak volumes. I remember the picture of Reverend Dozier on the Berkshire Eagle cover—hands straight, fingers unbent, crossed in front of her chest. That picture spoke of her strength, spoke of her faith, spoke of her humility, and acceptance of goodwill.

As for the A. M. E. Zion Church, five clergy offered prayers and remarks, emphasizing the spiritual side of Esther's life. They were followed by brief remarks from five individuals who had worked with Esther on her various humanitarian and heritage projects. The Price Memorial A. M. E. Zion Choir then brought the mourners back to the religious nature of the gathering. Bishop George A. Battle Jr., the presiding prelate of the Northeastern Episcopal District, delivered the eulogy, a powerful and emotional message that again made clear the central role that God played in Esther's life. Burial was at Elmwood Cemetery followed by a repast at the Berkshire South Regional Community Center.

While the funeral marked the end of Esther Dozier's life and the beginning of a new era for the Clinton Church, memorials to Esther and her life continued. Four days before the funeral, on 14 June 2007 the Massachusetts State Senate, on Senator Downing's motion, adjourned for the day at 12:06 pm in memory of "Reverend Esther Dozier." A month later, on 13 July, the American Boys Choir performed at the Mahaiwe Performing Arts Center, "In Memory of Rev. Esther Dozier, Pastor of Clinton A. M. E. Zion Church." Also in July, Albert Gordon, a civil rights activist and collector of indigenous art, donated a heart-shaped candle stand to the church. The stand was placed in the front of the Clinton sanctuary and was used in fundraising for the Esther Dozier Scholarship Fund, with candles lit to mark donations. The scholarship fund was established at the request of Esther's family, first suggested by her sister Pearl.

The formal memorials concluded a year later, on 11 June 2008, the one-year anniversary of her death, when a prayer service was held at the Clinton Church. Presentations were made by members of the church and representatives of the Great Barrington faith community including Rev. Joseph Forte and Rev. Mattie Conway of the Macedonia Baptist Church,

Rev. David Rogers of the United Methodist Church, Rev. Annie Ryder of the United Church of Christ, Rev. Willard H. Durant of the Price Memorial A. M. E. Zion Church, Roger Inhoff (retired Lutheran minister), Mel Greenberg of the Interfaith Council, and State Senator Ben Downing.

As noted, Rev. Dozier's death marked the end and the beginning of distinct phases in the Clinton Church's history. She had been active in the church for four decades and its pastor for nearly nine years. As we have outlined, with her encouragement and then her leadership the church had been a center of social activism to help the poor and homeless, and a strong and active supporter of the Upper Housatonic Valley African American Heritage Trail and the W. E. B. Du Bois Homesite projects. What the church's future would be was unknown but everyone knew it surely was going to be quite different.

Clinton Church Decline

Although it was not well known by those outside the church, the Clinton Church had continued to survive as a place of worship largely because of Esther and Henry's dedication and hard work. The membership was small and Esther and Henry, their two sons, daughters-in-law, and grandchildren made up about half the number who attended the weekly Sunday service. And the church's finances were precarious, as they had usually been for the church's entire existence. Thus, the Northeast Conference faced the questions of whether or not to keep the church open and whether or not to assign a new, full-time pastor. For several months, Louise Williamson, a close friend of Esther Dozier and deacon of the Price Memorial A. M. E. Zion Church in Pittsfield, and Mattie Conway, assistant pastor of the Macedonia Baptist Church around the corner, conducted services or services were held jointly with Macedonia. From six to twenty people attended the services at Clinton.

In September, Rev. Melvin Davis, assistant pastor of the Spottswood A. M. E. Zion Church in New Britain, was appointed Clinton's new pastor. Davis would continue living in Hartford and commute to Great Barrington for Sunday services and occasional Wednesday evening Bible study, a plan that proved somewhat ambitious given the Berkshires cold and snowy winters. Rev. Davis's tenure lasted a year and was difficult. In fairness, no one could have replaced Esther Dozier and Rev. Davis was not a good fit for the small, rural church. His style was very different, he did not live in town, and he took a more insular, inward-looking approach to the church's role in community life.

In 2009, Rev. Davis was reassigned and Rev. Louise Williamson, now ordained, took over as pastor. She did not live in town and commuted from Pittsfield. But, unlike Rev. Davis, she and her family had deep ties in the Berkshires and she was one of Esther's closest friends. Thus her appointment was greeted with a sigh of relief and the hope of stability and revitalization. But, as Rev. Davis had found, being an outsider, commuting for Sunday services, and being accepted as Ether Dozier's replacement in what was still Esther Dozier's church was really impossible. Her tenure lasted into 2011 and with no replacement named, the church no longer had a pastor, with members sometimes leading services, the last one in 2014. Short of not just a pastor but also members, attendees, and money, the building fell into disuse and disrepair. Paint peeled from the siding, holes opened in the roof, mold grew on the walls, and the basement was now permanently damp. With the church no longer functioning, it was decommissioned by the district.

While the Clinton Church had its own issues contributing to its decline, some context is required for a fuller understanding. The Clinton Church is one of four downtown Great Barrington churches that have closed since 2010 as religious affiliation seemed to decline with the three older, Main Street churches being sold, renovated, and repurposed for other uses more appealing to the town's and the region's affluent population. St. James (Episcopal) Church, founded in 1762, was sold in 2010 when the church could not afford extensive repairs needed for the slate roof and locally quarried blue dolomite walls and is now a cultural and arts center. In 2013, the Christian Science Church located in the historic Indiola Place villawas sold to McTeigue & McClelland Jewelers. That same year the United Methodist Church around the corner from Clinton was sold to developers planning a restaurant complex. This leaves the First Congregational and St. Peters Catholic as the only churches on Main Street, a street selected regularly as one of the best or the best main street in America.

A Center of African American Heritage

Despite the church's obstacles and difficulties, one initiative that did continue to flourish was Esther Dozier's vigorous and successful work to make the church an active participant in African American heritage projects in the region and a venue for events celebrating local and regional African American heritage and W. E. B. Du Bois. That initiative continued under her successor pastors, with trustee Wray Gunn the driving force, typically acting as the liaison between the church and the outside organizations, including the Upper Housatonic Valley African American Heritage Trail, the University of Massachusetts at Amherst, and the Friends of the Du Bois Homesite. Beyond helping to continue the work on African American heritage in the region, these events provided additional benefit to the church through the much-needed supplemental income gained from donations from attendees as well as donations to the Dozier Scholarship Fund.

In 2008, the Clinton Church gained additional recognition when it was placed on the Register of National Historic Places. Esther Dozier had initiated the application process in 2007 and on 12 March 2008 the process moved forward when the church was nominated by the Massachusetts Historical Commission.

Continuing its advocacy for the Du Bois legacy, in October 2009 the church hosted the "40th Anniversary of the W. E. B. Du Bois Boyhood Homesite and Memorial Park Dedication (October 18, 1969)." A moving vocal selection was offered by ethnomusicologist MaryNell Morgan of Empire State College and updates on plans for the Homesite development were provided by Jay Schafer, head of the University of Massachusetts at Amherst libraries (the university owns the property), and museum and exhibit designer Michael Singer.

On 27 February 2010, the church continued the practice of hosting a celebration of its founding, this year celebrating its 142nd birthday. The guest speaker was historian Gene Dattel, author of *Cotton and Race in the Making of America: The Human Costs of Economic Power* (2009).

In October 2010, the church again hosted a Du Bois event, this time a celebration of his life and contributions, with presentations by three female African American scholars: MaryNell Morgan, historian Francis Jones-Sneed of Massachusetts College of Liberal Arts, and historical archaeologist Whitney Battle-Baptiste of the University of Massachusetts at Amherst. A final Du Bois event took place on 19 February 2011, with a "Du Bois Gospel Birthday Tribute" celebrated by a performance by the Women of Faith Ensemble from St. John's Congregational Church in Springfield.

After this, with no pastor, the building falling into disrepair, and with several heritage sites along the Upper Housatonic Valley African American Trail now serving as venues for events, the Clinton Church's role as a venue for these events came to an end.

Clinton Church Restoration

Rarely used since 2012 and not at all since 2014, the church was decommissioned by the Northeastern District and fell into disrepair so severe it was no longer useable or even safe and had become an eyesore in Great Barrington's upscale downtown. On 7 June 2016, the district put the property up for sale with an asking price of $119,900. The fear among some in the community—former members, those involved in regional African American heritage, social activists, and admirers of Rev. Dozier—was that a new owner would most likely tear down the historically significant building and use the property as a parking lot, a precious commodity in tourist-happy Great Barrington.

Those deeply concerned about the church's demise and wishing to prevent its demolition quickly came together, meeting with the realtor and a representative of the district before the property was publicly listed for sale. The group, led at first by historian David Glassberg and archaeologist Robert Paynter of the University of Massachusetts at Amherst, and Dan Bolognani, executive director of the Upper Housatonic Valley National Heritage Area (UHVNHA), came together with the goal of working with any party interested in purchasing the building to ensure its survival, perhaps as an arts or cultural center. The group interested in saving the church quickly expanded to include local politicians and social activists and by November had coalesced into a formal non-profit organization, the Clinton Church Restoration (CCR). CCR was led by Wray Gunn, a long-time member and trustee of the Clinton Church and advocate of both African American heritage in the Berkshires and the legacy of W. E. B. Du Bois. Wray worked with a board of directors composed of local and regional individuals and an advisory board of historians, clergy, education experts, preservations, and other experts. CCR partnered with the UHVNHA and drew support from other organizations and business including The Triplex, the Great Barrington Historical Society, Multicultural Bridge, the Berkshire Clergy Association, and the University of Massachusetts at Amherst. CCR's goal was clear and ambitious:

The goal of the restoration project is to purchase, preserve and restore the decommissioned church for community use in a manner that celebrates and honors the local African American community, W.E.B. Du Bois' legacy, Great Barrington's history, African American spiritual tradition, and the work of the late Reverend Esther Dozier.

CCR moved quickly and by the end of the month had signed a purchase agreement for the property with a tentative closing scheduled for 30 March 2017. The board's first challenge toward reaching its goal was to save the building so there would be something to restore. The problem was the roof, which was likely to collapse during a snowy winter. That repair was completed in December when the roof was covered by a tarp, which along with the furring strips was donated by Herrington's building materials store of Sheffield, while the lift was provided by Taylor Rental, and the labor by local roofers.

The building was purchased on schedule and board of the Clinton Church Restoration expressed its commitment to education, religion, and community service, thereby keeping alive the church's long and rich legacy. To learn more about current activities, visit http://gbclintonchurch.org.

Sources

The two most important sources for this history are the church's own records, which date back to 1936, and Great Barrington's weekly newspaper, the *Berkshire Courier*. Information in these two has been supplemented by interviews with church members and other Great Barrington residents, town records, and other documents, many of which are located in the local history room of the town's Mason Library. Also of importance was Bernard Drew's 1999 town history, which provided much context and clarification. Similarly, my work as editor of *African American Heritage in the Upper Housatonic Valley* lent further context for the church's history.

As mentioned, records kept by the church exist for 1936 onward. I could find no records for any years prior to 1936, although they likely did and perhaps do still exist in some unknown location. The church records include a number of different items, not all of which are present for each year. They include annual membership books, which record weekly church attendance and dues payments; ledgers showing expenses and income; Quarterly Conference reports; journals of the chorus; journals of the Progressive Club; journals of the Jolly Club #12; letters written by church officials and those received by the church; materials relating to the NAACP; materials relating to the United Church Women; membership information sheets; annual budgets and financial reports; bank books; receipts; baptism lists; weekly programs; newspaper announcements; calendars; and other documents.

The *Berkshire Courier* was Great Barrington's weekly newspaper. It was not just a source of news but also a medium for communication. Although coverage of the church was less thorough than that for the white churches, there are very few years when some church activities were not mentioned, and major church developments often merited front-page coverage. Obituaries were a major source of personal information about church members. There was also occasional coverage in the daily *Berkshire Eagle.*

Reverend Esther Dozier and former Trustee Board chairman Wray Gunn were key sources of information for the 1950s on. Local historian Bernie Drew, Rachel Fletcher, Henry Dozier, Elaine Gunn, Leila Parrish, and Bobbie Wheeler, all long-time residents of Great Barrington, provided additional information.

Great Barrington town records, including vital records, annual reports, and reports of the school committee, yielded information about individuals. Deeds allowed me to trace the purchase and sale of the two properties owned by the church, mortgages, as well as property acquisitions and sales by church members. Editions of the *Southern Berkshire Directory* also provided information about church members, including where they lived and their occupations.

The Mason Library houses several files of material relevant to the church's history. These comprise early records of the Congregational churches in Great Barrington and Egremont and the Episcopal Church in Great Barrington; a history of Construct, Inc.; cemetery records; and miscellaneous clippings.

Bibliography

1907–1908 Resident and Business Directory of Southern Berkshire County, Mass. 1907. Great Barrington and Beverly, MA: Crowley & Lunt.

1910–1911 Resident and Business Directory of Southern Berkshire County, Mass. and the Township of North Canaan, Conn. 1910. Great Barrington and Beverly, MA: Crowley & Lunt.

1913–1914 Resident and Business Directory of Southern Berkshire County, Mass. and the Township of North Canaan, Conn. 1913. Great Barrington and Beverly, MA: Crowley & Lunt.

Berkshire Courier. 1861–1995. [Various articles and announcements.] Great Barrington, MA.

Broderick, F. L. 1959. *W. E. B. Du Bois: Negro Leader in a Time of Crisis.* Stanford, CA: Stanford University Press.

Brooks, Constance N. 2005. "Muddy Waters: W. E. B. Du Bois and the Commemorative Controversy over his Hometown's Symbolic Landscape." Master's diss., Department of Geography, Royal Holloway, University of London.

Brooks, Joanna. 2003. *American Lazarus: Religion and the Rise of African-American and Native American Literatures.* New York: Oxford University Press.

Brown, K. O. 1992. *Holy Ground: A Study of the American Camp Meeting.* New York: Garland.

Bureau of the Census, U.S. Department of Commerce and Labor. 1910. *Special Reports, Religious Bodies: 1906. Part I Summary and General Tables.* Washington: Government Printing Office.

Chapman, Gerard. No date. "A History of Construct Inc.; 1969–1979." Mason Library, Great Barrington, MA.

Child, H., comp. 1885. *Gazetteer of Berkshire County, Mass. 1725–1885.* Syracuse, NY: Journal Office.

Consolati, Florence. 1978. *See All the People; or, Life in Lee.* Lee, MA: privately printed.

Doughton, Thomas L. 1999. *Men Listing Massachusetts Towns as Their Place of Residence Who Enlisted in the 54th Regiment.* Retrieved 8 August 2005, from http://www.geocities.com/afroyankees/Military/54mass2.html

Drew, Bernard A. 1999. *Great Barrington: Great Town/Great History.* Great Barrington, MA: Great Barrington Historical Society.

Drew, Bernard A. 2002. *Fifty Sites in Great Barrington, Massachusetts Associated with the Civil Rights Activist W. E. B. Du Bois.* Great Barrington, MA: Great Barrington Historical Society.

Drew, Bernard A. 2004. "Willoughby's Sunset Inn." *Berkshire Eagle,* 22 May, A7.

Drew, Bernard A. 2004. *If They Close the Door on You, Go in the Window: Origins of the African American Community in Sheffield, Great Barrington and Stockbridge.* Great Barrington: Attic Revivals Press.

Du Bois, W. E. B. 1883–1885. "Early Writings." [Columns from the *New York Independent.*] Reprinted in Julius Lester, ed. 1971. *The Seventh Son: The Thought and Writings of W. E. B. Du Bois.* New York: Vintage Books, vol. 1, 154–169.

Du Bois, W. E .B. 1898. *The Philadelphia Negro: A Social Study.* Philadelphia: University of Pennsylvania Press.

Du Bois, W. E. B. 1903. *The Souls of Black Folk: Essays and Sketches.* Chicago: A. C. McClurg.

Du Bois, W. E. B., ed. 1903. *The Negro Church.* Atlanta, GA: Atlanta University Press.

Du Bois, W. E. B. 1920. *Darkwater: Voices from within the Veil.* New York: Harcourt, Brace & Howe.

Du Bois, W. E. B. 1935. *Black Reconstruction.* New York: Russell & Russell.

Du Bois, W. E. B. 1968. *The Autobiography of W. E. B. Du Bois.* New York: International Publishers.

Du Bois, W. E. B. 1986. *The Suppression of the African Slave Trade to the United States of America 1638–1870.* New York: Library of America. Ph.D. thesis, Harvard University, 1896.

"Early Records of the Congregational Church." Typed manuscript at the Mason Library, Great Barrington, MA.

Emilio, Luis F. 1894. *History of the Fifty-Fourth Regiment of Massachusetts Volunteer Infantry, 1863–1865.* Boston: Boston Book Co.

First Resistance Chapter, N.S.D.A.R. 1935–1938. "Tombstone Inscriptions Great Barrington, Massachusetts." Typed manuscript at the Mason Library, Great Barrington, MA.

Gentile, Derek. 2006. "Religions Differ, but Message Stays the Same." *Berkshire Eagle,* 19 March , 1, 5.

Great Barrington, Town of. 1865–1895. *Annual Reports of the Officers of the Town of Great Barrington, Berkshire County, Massachusetts.* Great Barrington, MA.

Great Barrington, Town of. 1894–1895, 1895–1896, 1896–1897. *Annual Reports of the School Committee of the Town of Great Barrington, Massachusetts.* Great Barrington, MA.

Great Barrington, Town of. 1871–1945. Registry of Deeds. Vol. 140: 323; vol. 157: 249–250; vol. 163: 70, 79, 320; vol. 190: 138, 222; vol. 197: 144–145; vol. 211: 356; vol. 215: 17; vol. 220: 111, 150–151; vol. 237: 62–63; vol. 277: 267.

Great Barrington Directory 1894–5. 1894. New Haven, CT: Price & Lee Co.

Harris, Meriah E. 1899. "Women in the Pioneer Work of the Church." *A. M. E. Zion Quarterly Review* (April).

History of Berkshire County, Massachusetts, with Biographical Sketches of Prominent Men. 1885. New York: J. B. Beers & Co.

Hood, James W. 1895. *One Hundred Years of the African Methodist Episcopal Zion Church; or, The Centennial of African Methodism.* New York: A. M. E. Zion Book Concern.

Hoog, Cynthia T. No date. "Death Notices from the Berkshire Courier 1834 through 1890." Unpublished report, on file at the Mason Library, Great Barrington, MA.

Hoog, Cynthia T. 1987. "Cemetery Inscriptions in Great Barrington, Massachusetts." Unpublished report, on file at the Mason Library, Great Barrington, MA.

Hyde, C. M., and A. Hyde. 1878. *The Centennial Celebration and Centennial History of the Town of Lee, Mass.* Springfield, MA: Clark W. Bryan and Co.

Levinson, David, ed. 2006. *African American Heritage in the Upper Housatonic Valley.* Great Barrington, MA: Berkshire Publishing Group.

Lewis, David Levering. 1993. *W. E. B. Du Bois: Biography of a Race, 1868–1919.* New York: Henry Holt.

Lincoln, C. Eric, and Lawrence H. Mamiya. 1990. *The Black Church in the African American Experience.* Durham, NC, and London: Duke University Press.

McHenry, Elizabeth. 2002. *Forgotten Readers; Recovering the Lost History of African American Literary Societies.* Durham, NC: Duke University Press.

Michaels, Julie. 1979. "AME Zion Comes of Age." *Berkshire Sampler,* 25 March.

Miller, James R. 2002. *Early Life in Sheffield, Berkshire County, Massachusetts.* Sheffield, MA: Sheffield Historical Society.

Muller, Nancy L. 2001. *W. E. B. Du Bois and the House of the Black Burghardts: Land, Family, and African Americans in New England.* Ph.D. diss., University of Massachusetts at Amherst.

Moore, J. J. 1884. *History of the A. M. E. Zion Church in America. Founded in 1796, in the City of New York.* York, PA: Teachers' Journal Offices.

Murphy, L. G.; J. G. Melton; and G. L. Ward, eds. 1993. *Encyclopedia of African American Religions.* New York: Garland.

Preiss, Lillian E. 1976. *Sheffield; Frontier Town.* Sheffield, MA: Sheffield Bicentennial Committee.

Records of Deaths, Kept by Rev. Sylvester Burt, of the Congregational Church. Typed manuscript at the Mason Library, Great Barrington, MA.

Southern Berkshire Directory, (including Canaan, Conn.) The. 1916. Vol. IV, 1916–1918. Great Barrington and Beverly, MA: Crowley & Lunt.

South Berkshire Directory, (including Canaan, Conn.) The. 1920. Vol. V, 1920–1921. Great Barrington and Beverly, MA: Crowley & Lunt.

Taylor, Charles A. 1928. *History of Great Barrington: Part I: 1676—1882.* (Original work published 1882). Great Barrington, MA: Town of Great Barrington.

Thorbrough, Emma Lou 1972. *T. Thomas Fortune: Militant Journalist.* Chicago: University of Chicago Press.

Transactions of the Housatonic Agricultural Society. 1859–1873. 1873. Springfield, MA: Samuel Bowles & Co., 19.

Tucker, Karen B. W. 2001. *American Methodist Worship.* New York: Oxford University Press.

Vital Records of Great Barrington, Massachusetts to the Year 1850. 1904. Boston: New England Historic Genealogical Society. Retrieved 8 July 2002, from

http://www.rootsweb.com/~maberksh/towns/greatbarr/grt_barr_birth.html

Walls, William J. 1974. *The African Methodist Episcopal Zion Church; Reality of the Black Church.* Charlotte, NC: A. M. E. Zion Publishing House.

Zuckerman, P., ed. 2000. *Du Bois on Religion.* Walnut Creek, CA: Altamira Press.

The Berkshire Eagle. 2007–2017. (Various articles). Pittsfield, MA.

Fletcher, Rachel. (2017). Personal communications with the author.

Bolognani, Dan. (2017). Personal communications with the author.

Pastors of the Clinton
A. M. E. Zion Church, 1870–2011

1870–1873	W. J. Dorsey	**1901**	Isaac Watkins
1873–N.A.	William B. Smith		John. I. W. D. LeChia
1880	Silas Mitchell	**1902**	John. I. W. D. LeChia
1881	Silas Mitchell		Isaac Watkins
1882	J. H. Anderson	**1903**	Isaac Watkins
1883	J. H. Anderson		W. B. Caine
1884	J. H. Anderson	**1904**	W. B. Caines
	J. F. Lloyd		J. A. Curtiss
1885	J. F. Lloyd	**1905**	J. A. Curtiss
	Joseph G. Smith		David R. Overton
1886	Joseph G. Smith	**1906**	David R. Overton
1887	Joseph G. Smith	**1907**	David R. Overton
	George H. Simmons	**1908**	David R. Overton
1888	J. F. Waters	**1909**	Samuel E. Robinson
1889	J. F. Waters	**1910**	Samuel E. Robinson
1890	J. F. Waters	**1911**	Samuel E. Robinson
	G. A. Given	**1912**	Samuel E. Robinson
1891	S. W. Hutchings		Samuel H. Johnson
1892	S. W. Hutchings	**1913**	Samuel H. Johnson
1893	S. W. Hutchings		John E. Hill
	Alfred Day	**1914**	John E. Hill
1894	Alfred Day		Sidney Smith
	Chauncey Hatfield	**1915**	Sidney Smith
1895	Chauncey Hatfield		B. W. Smith
1896	Chauncey Hatfield	**1916**	B. W. Smith
	C. O. Waters	**1917**	B. W. Smith
1897	C. O. Waters		Byron Scott
	W. H. Parker	**1918**	Byron Scott
1898	W. H. Parker	**1919**	Byron Scott
	James H. Young	**1920**	Byron Scott
1899	James H. Young		William H. Martin
	Isaac Watkins	**1921**	William H. Martin
1900	Isaac Watkins		Byron Scott

1922	Byron Scott	1947	Raleigh Dove
1923	Byron Scott	1948	Raleigh Dove
1924	Byron Scott	1949	Raleigh Dove
1925	Byron Scott	1950	Raleigh Dove
	J. C. McRae	1951	Raleigh Dove
1926	J. C. McRae		Luther A. Holloway
	Byron Scott		Alexander W. Johnson
1927	Byron Scott	1952	Alexander W. Johnson
	J. C. McRae	1953	Alexander W. Johnson
1928	J. C. McRae	1954	Alexander W. Johnson
	Byron Scott		David Woodson
1929	E. H. Raynor	1955	David Woodson
1930	E. H. Raynor	1956	David Woodson
1931	Byron Scott	1957	David Woodson
	Uriah Bertrand		N. Randolph Scott
1932	Uriah Bertrand	1958	N. Randolph Scott
	Edward W. Gantt		William A. Kelley
1933	Edward W. Gantt	1959	William A. Kelley
	Maurice T. Joseph	1960	William A. Kelley
1934	Maurice T. Joseph	1961	William A. Kelley
	I. B. Walters	1962	William A. Kelley
1935	I. B. Walters		William E. Durante
1936	I. B. Walters	1963	William E. Durante
	Edward H. Coleman	1964	William E. Durante
1937	Edward H. Coleman	1965	William E. Durante
1938	Edward H. Coleman	1966	William E. Durante
1939	Edward H. Coleman	1967	William E. Durante
1940	Edward H. Coleman	1968	William E. Durante
	Henry W. Morrison	1969	William E. Durante
1941	Henry W. Morrison	1970	William E. Durante
1942	Henry W. Morrison	1971	William E. Durante
1943	Henry W. Morrison	1972	William E. Durante
1944	Henry W. Morrison		James Little
1945	Henry W. Morrison	1973	James Little
	George F. Green	1974	James Little
1946	George F. Green	1975	James Little
	Raleigh Dove		Douglas E. Lawrence

1976	Douglas E. Lawrence	**1994**	John R. Parron
	John Cooper	**1995**	John R. Parron
1977	John Cooper	**1996**	John R. Parron
1978	John Cooper	**1997**	John R. Parron
1979	John Cooper	**1998**	John R. Parron
1980	John Cooper	**1999**	John R. Parron
1981	John Cooper		Esther Dozier
1982	John Cooper	**2000**	Esther Dozier
1983	James B. Hubert	**2001**	Esther Dozier
1984	James B. Hubert	**2002**	Esther Dozier
1985	James B. Hubert	**2003**	Esther Dozier
1986	James B. Hubert	**2004**	Esther Dozier
1987	James B. Hubert	**2005**	Esther Dozier
1988	James B. Hubert	**2006**	Esther Dozier
	Samuel W. Henderson	**2007**	Melvin Davis
1989	John R. Parron	**2008**	Melvin Davis
1990	John R. Parron	**2009**	Louise Williamson
1991	John R. Parron	**2010**	Louise Williamson
1992	John R. Parron	**2011**	Louise Williamson
1993	John R. Parron		

Clinton Church Restoration's goal is to save, preserve, and repurpose the former Clinton A.M.E. Zion Church at 9 Elm Court in downtown Great Barrington. Once preserved, the historic property will be a vital, self-sustaining entity for community use that celebrates and honors its first female pastor, Rev. Esther Dozier; the local African American community; and the legacy of W.E.B. Du Bois. The 130-year-old church, now deconsecrated, is listed on the National Register of Historic Places and is a site on the Upper Housatonic Valley African American Heritage Trail.

http://gbclintonchurch.org/

CLINTON CHURCH
RESTORATION

Index

About the Author

David Levinson is a cultural anthropologist. He has been the editor or senior editor of several major anthropological reference works including the *Encyclopedia of World Cultures*, the *Encyclopedia of Cultural Anthropology*, and *American Immigrant Groups*. He received his PhD at SUNY/Buffalo; his research has focused on cross-cultural studies, forgotten or invisible peoples, family relationships, ethnic relations, and local history and culture. He is the author of *African American Heritage in the Upper Housatonic Valley*, among other books. Levinson was formerly vice-president of the Human Relations Area Files, at Yale University, and was a co-founder of Berkshire Publishing Group in Great Barrington, Massachusetts, the hometown of W. E. B. Du Bois.